Chris Stewart

DRIVING
OVER LEMONS

Chris Stewart lives in Spain with his wife, Ana,
and his daughter, Chloë.

DRIVING
OVER LEMONS

DRIVING
OVER LEMONS

～

AN OPTIMIST IN SPAIN

Chris Stewart

VINTAGE DEPARTURES

Vintage Books

A Division of Random House, Inc.

New York

 FIRST VINTAGE DEPARTURES EDITION, MAY 2001

Copyright © 1999 by Chris Stewart

The Library of Congress has cataloged the Pantheon edition as follows:
Stewart, Chris, 1951–
Driving over lemons : an optimist in Andalucía / Chris Stewart
p. cm.
ISBN: 0-375-41028-7
1. Alpujarra Region (Spain)—Description and travel.   2. Alpujarra
Region (Spain)—Social life and customs.   3. Stewart, Chris, 1951—
homes and haunts—Spain—Alpujarra Region.   4. Country life—
Spain—Alpujarra Region.   I. Title
DP302.A38 S74 2000
946'.8—dc21 99-056675

Vintage ISBN: 0-375-70915-0

Author photograph © Andrew Crowley/Camera Press/Retna, Ltd.

www.vintagebooks.com

Printed in the United States of America
10   9   8

CONTENTS

v

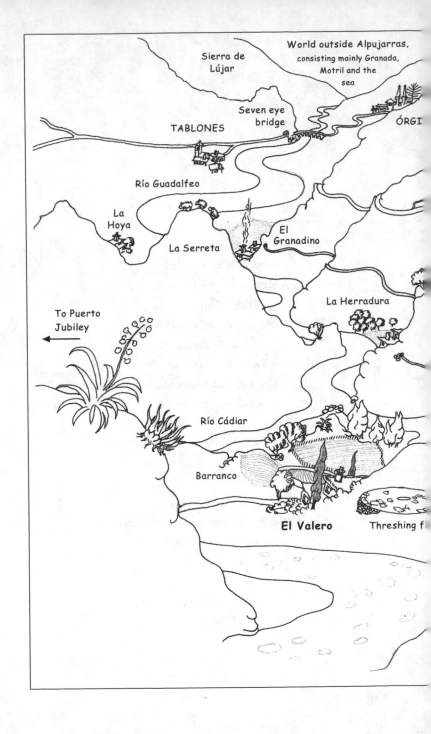

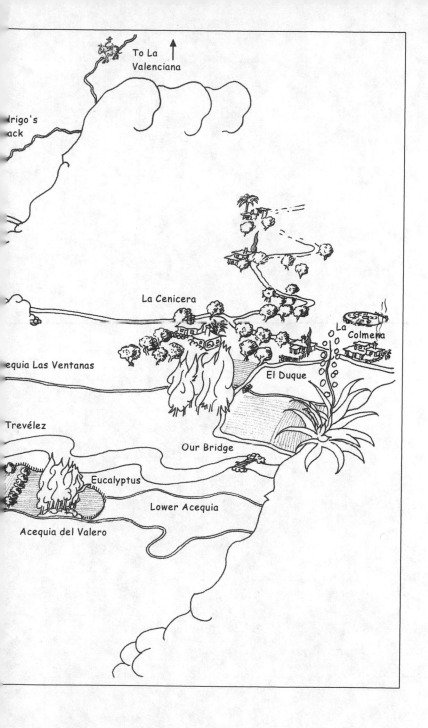

To La
Valenciana

drigo's
ack

La Cenicera

La
Colmena

El Duque

equia Las Ventanas

Trevélez

Our Bridge

Eucalyptus

Lower Acequia

Acequia del Valero

DRIVING
OVER LEMONS

EL VALERO

'WELL, THIS IS NO GOOD, I DON'T WANT TO LIVE HERE!' I
said as we drove along yet another tarmac road behind a row
of whitewashed houses. 'I want to live in the mountains, for
heaven's sake, not in the suburbs of some town in a valley.'

'Shut up and keep driving,' ordered Georgina, the woman sitting beside me. She lit another cigarette of strong black tobacco
and bathed me in a cloud of smoke.

I'd only met Georgina that afternoon but it hadn't taken her
long to put me in my place. She was a confident young
Englishwoman with a peculiarly Mediterranean way of seeming
at ease with her surroundings. For the last ten years she had been
living in the Alpujarras, the foothills of the Sierra Nevada, south
of Granada, and she had carved out a niche for herself acting as
an intermediary between the farmers who wanted to sell their
cortijos in the hills and move to town, and the foreigners who
wanted to buy them. It was a tough job but no one who saw her

1

ironing out deals with the coarsest peasant or arguing water rights with the most stubborn bureaucrat could doubt she was the woman for it. If she had a weakness at all it was in her refusal to suffer fools and ditherers.

'Do you bully all your clients like this?' I protested.

'No, just you. Left here.'

Obediently I turned the wheel and we shrugged off the last houses of Órgiva, the market town where I'd been adopted by my agent. We bumped onto a dirt track and headed downhill towards the river.

'Where are the mountains?' I whined.

Georgina ignored me and looked at the groves of oranges and olives on either side of the track. There were white houses covered in the scrags of last year's vines and decked with bright geraniums and bougainvillea; mules were ploughing; boiler-suited growers were bent bum-up amid perfect lines of vegetables; a palm tree shaded the road where hens were swimming in the dust. Dogs slept in the road in the shade; cats slept in the road in the sun. The creature with lowest priority on the road was the car. I stopped and backed up a bit to go round a lemon.

'Drive over lemons,' ordered Georgina.

There were, it was true, a hell of a lot of lemons. They hurtled past, borne on a stream of water that bubbled nearby; in places the road was a mat of mashed fruit, and the earth beneath the trees was bright with fallen yellow orbs. I remembered a half-forgotten snatch of song, something about a lovelorn gypsy throwing lemons into the Great River until it turned to gold.

The lemons, the creatures and the flowers warmed my heart a little. We drove on through a flat plain quilted with cabbages and beans, at the end of which loomed a little mountain. After dipping a banana grove, we turned sharp right up a steep hill with deep cuttings in the red rock.

'This looks more like it.'

2

'Just wait, we're not there yet.'

Up and up we went, bend after bend, the river valley spread below us like an aerial print. On through a gorge and suddenly we burst into a new valley. The plain we had crossed disappeared utterly, hidden from sight by the mass of mountain, and drowned by the roaring of the river in the gorge below.

Far below, beside the river, I caught sight of a little farm in a horseshoe-shaped valley, a derelict house on a cactus-covered crag, surrounded by unkempt fields and terraces of ancient olive trees.

'La Herradura,' Georgina announced. 'What about that, then?'

'Well, it's nice to dream but the pittance we've got to spend is hardly going to buy us a place like that.'

'With the money you've got to spend you could afford that place and have some left over to do it up.'

'I don't believe you. You can't possibly be serious.'

I was incredulous because this was so far beyond my wildest hopes. I had come to Spain with a sum of money that would barely stretch to a garden shed in the south of England, expecting to buy at best a ruined house with perhaps a little patch of land.

'Well, there's no point in going any further. I'll have that one. Let's go down and see it.'

We pulled the car off the road and tripped down a path. I was so overwhelmed with excitement and delight that I felt sick. I picked an orange from a tree, the first time I'd ever done that. It was quite the most disgusting orange I'd ever eaten.

'Sweet oranges,' said Georgina. 'They're mostly sweet oranges here – good for juice. And the old men with no teeth like them.'

'This is it, Georgina. It's paradise. I want it. I mean, I'll buy it now.'

'It's not a good idea to be too hasty in these matters. Let's go and have a look at some other places.'

3

'I don't want to see anywhere else. I want to live here, and anyway I'm your client. Surely we do what I want, not what you want!'

We drove off, further into the valley, and Georgina took me to see a stone ruin that was slowly slithering down a hill towards a precipice. It was surrounded by rotting cactus, and groves of dead trees covered the dismal hill around it. A poisonous spring oozed from a clump of thorns at the bottom of the property.

'Hell no, what did you want me to see that place for?'

'It has its good points.'

'It has the advantage of being a long way from the nearest golf course, but more than that I cannot see.'

We moved on to look at a concrete blockhouse, a battery chicken shed, a filthy hovel infested with bats, and a sort of cave littered with turds and old bits of newspaper.

'I don't want to see any more of this sort of thing. Let's go back to La Herradura.'

So we did, and I sat on a warm stone in the riverbed, dreaming one of those rare dreams that suddenly start to materialise around you, until Georgina intruded.

'I know it's very nice, Chris, but there are problems with La Herradura. It's owned by a number of people, and they don't all want to sell – and one of those who doesn't want to sell has access to a room he owns right plumb in the middle of the house. That could be inconvenient if not downright disagreeable. And then there's the matter of the water . . .'

Her words faded as we both turned our heads to catch a snatch of song rolling towards us along the riverbed. I made out the words 'frog' and 'crystal glasses' but the rest was lost in a gruff baritone. From behind a rock came a red goat with only one horn. It eyed us up for a moment, then performed that trick that has so endeared the goat to mankind since the beginnings of time, the simultaneous belch and fart.

4

'Clever the way they do that, isn't it?'

Georgina ignored this observation. 'The man you see approaching us now,' she announced in an urgent whisper, 'is the owner of the place across the river – and I think that he may want to sell it.'

Following the one-horned goat came a huge man with a red bristly face, sitting astride a horse. He was doing the singing, presumably to amuse himself while he supervised the goat and its several companions, who included a couple of cows, a kid, a grubby sheep and a pair of dogs. He stopped, lurched forward in his saddle and surveyed us from beneath a filthy cotton beach-hat. With an oath he halted his entourage.

'Hola, buenas tardes. Would you be Pedro Romero, he who owns the farm across the river?' began Georgina.

The man grunted.

'I've heard you may want to sell it.'

'Maybe I do.'

'Then we want to come and see it.'

'When?'

'Tomorrow morning.'

'I'll be there.'

'How do we get there?'

There followed a long-winded explanation of which I could only catch the odd reference to trees, brambles and stones. All rather unnecessary, I thought, as we were looking at the farm not half a mile away.

'This foreigner wants to buy the place?' He leered at me, assessing my worth.

'Maybe he does, maybe he doesn't.'

'Till tomorrow, then.'

'Till tomorrow.'

With which the little procession jangled its way back down the river. Romero had stopped singing and appeared lost in thought.

5

I watched entranced as the lowering sun lit the little clouds of golden dust raised by the animals' feet.

'I know a thing or two about this business,' Georgina said, 'and that farm is definitely worth a look. It's called El Valero.'

~

Georgina considered me thoughtfully as we drank a morning coffee together before setting out for the valley.

'Listen, you're to keep quiet unless I prompt you. Leave the talking to me.'

'Alright. But hang on. Have we actually established that I want to buy El Valero? I was under the impression, if you'll forgive me, that I wanted La Herradura.'

Georgina looked me squarely in the eye. 'I've given the matter some thought, and I've decided that El Valero and you are well suited. You'll see when we get there.'

We drove to the valley in warm January sunshine. The farmers were working their fields of vegetables, the dogs and cats had returned to their allotted places in the road. It looked familiar this time. As we passed La Herradura, I looked down at it wistfully, and then with some misgivings at the place across the river.

After a while the road gave out completely, and we took our shoes off and waded through the river, which was knee-deep and fast-running in places, not to say cold. 'This is a hell of a way to get to a place,' I shouted, 'if you'll excuse my saying so.'

We climbed up a bank by eucalyptus trees and across a field, and from there followed a narrow path through terraces shot with flowers and shaded by oranges, lemons and olives. Clear runnels of water flowed here and there, tumbling down stony falls and spreading to water terraces of fruit trees and vegetables. The path stepped across a stream and curled up through a grove of blossoming almonds. Georgina turned and smiled at me.

'What do you think?'

'You know what I think – I've never seen anything like it!'

'Here's the house.'

'House?! It looks like a whole village. I can't buy a village.'

A couple of houses with some stables and goat-pens, chicken-runs and store-rooms, were spread at different levels on a great steep rock. Beneath this complex a hose dribbled feebly into a rusty oil-drum by a pomegranate tree.

Pedro Romero stood beside what was either a house or a stable, rubbing his hands and grinning.

'Ha! You've come. Sit down and drink wine, eat meat!'

We sat on low chairs with our knees up by our ears, and enjoyed the spectacle of two dogs copulating enthusiastically in the centre of the circle made by the seats. I didn't know whether it would be appropriate to offer some ribald comment upon this activity, or to pretend that it was not happening. Georgina glowered at me and I kept quiet as agreed.

A wizened wisp of a woman appeared, Romero's wife, Maria, and at an imperious gesture from the man of the house dispensed brown wine from a plastic Coca-Cola bottle and thumped a fatty lump of ham down on the box that served for a table. The sun shone down, flies buzzed. We drank the wine and ate the ham and considered the amorous activities of the dogs in an increasingly vinous stupor.

Georgina and Romero talked animatedly about neighbours and boundaries and water and rates and rights while I rocked back and forth on my chair and grinned vacuously. The dogs were quiet now as a result of being stuck together, looking bashfully in opposite directions, wishing perhaps that they'd never started the whole wretched business. The wine and the ham came and went, and I nodded off, then opened a heavy-lidded eye as Georgina poked me in the ribs.

'Slap this into his hand as if you mean it.'

7

She passed me a fat wad of peseta notes of large denomination. 'You're now the happy owner of El Valero and that's the *señal* – the deposit.'

It really was no use arguing with Georgina so I did as she said and bought the place. There was a deal of backslapping, hand-shaking and grinning all round.

'It was a gift at that price,' lamented Romero and his wife. 'We're ruined, really we've given our home away . . . you've bought a paradise for pennies, but what could we do?'

I almost began to offer them more money but Georgina shot me a silencing look, and so, for a little under five million pesetas (£25,000, more or less), I had bought a farm that I would have hardly dared look at over the fence before. In a matter of minutes I was transformed from an itinerant sheep-shearer and tenant of a tied cottage beneath an airport landing path in Sussex, into the owner of a mountain farm in Andalucía. This would take some getting used to.

~

Barely able to contain my excitement I drove to the nearest bar to phone Ana, my wife, in England – and there pulled up short. How exactly was I going to explain to her what I had just done? I shuffled the coins about on the table and looked for inspiration at the dregs in my wineglass. Strictly speaking, my brief had been to check out certain places in Andalucía and look at the possibility of buying a house and plot of land where together we could carve out a future. I couldn't help but feel that I had somewhat overstepped the mark. There comes a tide in the affairs of men, of course . . . but would Ana see it in quite that light?

She didn't. But then, in her position, neither probably would I. However, fortunately for us both, Ana has never been one for recriminations, and she soon shifted into that cautious line of enquiry that doctors employ after arriving at the scene of an accident.

'How far is it from the nearest road?' was her first question. It was a relief to be dealing with the practicalities.

'Oh, it's just about the distance from the cottage to the piggery.' I tried to imagine Ana looking across the Sussex farmyard. 'And that's not far, is it? I mean it's not very far to the piggery . . . No, there's no running water . . . wait, I tell a lie – there's a babbling hosepipe tied to an oil-drum about twenty metres below the house.'

I talked at length of the scarlet geranium petals floating on the water of the drum, of the gentle beasts stooping to drink, and of the bright flowers that carpeted the ground around this lovely pool. But Ana was not to be side-tracked.

'Yes, as a matter of fact there is a bathroom, and it has a bidet, too . . . No, admittedly the water doesn't reach there . . . the spring's not high enough, you see . . . if you raise the hosepipe above the drum it stops dribbling, er, running . . . No, you can't drink it, it's poisonous. They don't wash in it either – they wash their hair in the river which is rather nice I think. They told me that if you water plants too much with it they die . . . No, I don't know why they put it there in the first place! I can't read their minds, can I? The beasts drink it – yes, that's it, the beasts drink it. And no, I don't know why the beasts don't drink from the river – presumably because people wash their hair in it!'

I was getting in deeper. I tried another tack.

'It has electricity – a solar panel, so you have no electricity bills and you can use as much as you like. They have a television and some lights, including a switch that turns the light on and off from the bed, would you believe? Apparently you have to be a little sparing with it in summer . . .

9

'In winter? Well, no, in winter I suppose it doesn't work at all, but then you can't have everything, can you?'

Ana, although not quite convinced by my romantic view of El Valero's charms, said she was prepared to accept all these nightmarish aspects just so long as it wasn't windy. Wind was the worst thing in the world to her.

'It's snuggled into a nice little nook in a river valley,' I assured her. In fact it isn't. El Valero stands on a ridge, vulnerable to the winds of two rivers and two great chains of mountains. Still, with that tiny adjustment of the truth, I was able to arouse Ana's enthusiasm to the point that she promised to keep an open mind when she arrived on the next available charter.

I meanwhile stayed on, viewing my new property from every aspect. I scrambled up to the top of the twin-peaked hill across the river and looked across the dry scrub and pines to where El Valero appeared a little oasis with its dark fruit trees and bright streams of water. I could see Romero sitting in the riverbed on his horse, surrounded by his ill-favoured beasts, and his wife and daughter, backs bent to the planting of a terrace of garlic.

I climbed up the steep ridge behind the farm, way up till I could no longer hear the river and was lost amid the rosemary and thyme, with just the sound of the wind in the broom and the cries of unfamiliar birds. From there I looked over the whole valley, which widened at one end to gently sloping green fields and orchards before disappearing altogether into the deep cleft in the mountain where the river came rushing through, and at the other narrowing to the rocky gorge at El Granadino, the little settlement at the southern end of the valley. The farm looked infinitesimally small at the foot of the great hill, with a hillock at its tip, like the horn on the nose of a rhinoceros.

In the softening light of the afternoon I drove high up onto the Contraviesa, the great counterscarp to the southwest, and found

10

a spot where I could see the whole valley, green and lovely and apparently inaccessible, lost amongst the dry hills of scrub and thorn.

My head was whirling with excitement; wild ideas and dreams pouring in. It was an amazing prospect. Every way I walked, and from each approach, I wondered at the beauty of the two rivers pouring into the wide valley, and the tall narrow gorge at its mouth. Then something began to dawn on me. This was a natural spot for a reservoir. A dam just fifty metres wide at the mouth of the gorge would fill the whole valley in weeks – two rivers, narrow gorge, just a few illiterate peasants to re-locate; the coastal towns just twenty kilometres south were dry as bricks, people drinking salty water from drying wells. It all fitted together. That was why everyone wanted to sell their farms. They'd be under water in a few years.

As this ghastly notion took hold, dark shadows started to shroud my new world. How the hell was I going to explain this to Ana? Even now, perhaps, she was scudding through the clouds towards the south of Spain. I ran dementedly down to the river to find Romero and his beasts.

'Are they going to build a dam here and flood the valley?'

My future – to say nothing of my marriage – depended upon his reply. He looked at me in some surprise, a cunning grin playing across his unlovely features.

'Of course.'

'Do you mean to tell me,' I squeaked, 'that you've just sold me a place that will be twenty metres under the surface of a reservoir in a couple of years' time?!'

'*Claro* – naturally.'

'How could you . . ?'

'Oh, you'll be alright, they'll pay you a whole heap of compensation for the place.'

'But I haven't bought it for the damn compensation, I want to live here . . . '

'That could well be difficult, under the water and that. But I must be off. I have to follow the beasts.'

And so saying, he whopped his horse with a stick and disappeared up the river.

PARADISE SUBMERGED

GEORGINA WAS LEANING ON A FRUIT MACHINE, READING A book about alchemy, when I burst into the Bar Retumba at the far end of town.

'Georgina, what the hell is all this about a dam?' I erupted.

'A dam? What dam?' She seemed genuinely puzzled.

'Pedro Romero has just told me that they're going to build a dam and flood the valley.'

'Oh, that.'

'What do you mean by "Oh, that!"?'

My look of anguish must have moved her, for she softened her tone a little. 'Well, yes, there was a plan about twenty-five years ago to put a dam across the gorge and flood the valley, but the tests they did showed that it couldn't be managed economically. The surrounding rock is like a sponge. And anyway, even if they do resurrect the scheme, you'll be well paid for your trouble. It really isn't a problem.'

'Can we be sure of that? I mean absolutely sure?'

She mulled this over for a moment before shutting her book and reaching for her bag.

'I'll tell you what, we'll go and see Domingo. He's your nearest neighbour in the valley. He lives at La Colmena, at the north end. His family have lived there for years. He's bound to know. I saw his car earlier so he must be around here somewhere.'

And she set off at her usual brisk pace along the main street of Órgiva, while I traipsed along in her wake.

'Keep your eyes open,' she ordered. 'He's easy to spot – one of the best-looking men you'll see round here. He's around thirty, short, but then so is everyone here, and balding a little . . . '

'Not the most promising of portraits,' I commented, feeling that I could be forgiven a little peevishness in the circumstances.

'Ah, just you wait and see. He's built like a prize fighter and has the loveliest smile you could imagine.' It seemed that the man had certainly worked some magic on Georgina.

Down we strode past the grandly named 'Museum of Ham', in reality just a small supermarket, past the town hall hung with its flags of Andalucía and Spain, and on to the main street and another cluster of bars.

Here we found my neighbour, leaning nonchalantly against a lamp post talking to a gypsy. He was trying to sell him a cow, or so it appeared. We waited to allow the transaction to reach some sort of conclusion, but it seemed to be a long time getting nowhere, both parties refusing absolutely to be swayed. A few bystanders had gathered round, keen to involve themselves in the deal. Georgina guided me to a bar across the street and signalled an invitation to Domingo to join us when he had finished his negotiations.

I watched Domingo from our table as he conducted his business. The other participants in the deal were listening with attention to what he had to say. He gave the impression of being accustomed to holding the floor. He was dressed in clean blue jeans, a white open-necked shirt and sneakers. The top of his head was, as Georgina had said, as bald as a shiny brown nut.

Eventually he came over to join us. He shook hands with a shy smile, studying some spot below the table as Georgina introduced us.

'Are you just going to come for holidays?' he asked.

'Hell no, we're going to live here and farm.'

At this Domingo smiled, momentarily lifting his head. Georgina was absolutely right. His expression was transformingly handsome.

'What do you know of the dam in the valley of La Colmena?' Georgina asked. 'Pedro Romero has been telling Cristóbal about some plans . . .'

'Don't listen to Romero,' said Domingo quietly. 'There was a project many years ago but it came to nothing. There's no danger of its being revived.'

'Are you sure about that?' I gabbled. 'You see, it's really very important to us. We want to live out our days there, not cash in on compensation.'

'Yes, of course I'm sure, but if you want to hear it from someone official we'll go and see the mayor.'

With little more preamble we set out. In his sneakers and jeans Domingo wandered straight through the open door of the mayor's office.

'Hola, Antonio. This foreigner, Cristóbal, has bought the farm next to La Colmena, and he's worried about the dam. I've told him, but I think he'd like to hear it from the mayor. You tell him.'

Antonio repeated all that Domingo had just told me. But by then I was no longer thinking of the dam. I was congratulating myself on landing such an estimable neighbour.

15

With this load off my mind, I collected Ana from the airport, skimming back towards Granada in the biscuit tin of a car that I had hired. We watched as the snowy peaks of the Sierra Nevada appeared from a blue haze above the city and the winter sun set the tops glowing rose pink with the last rays of the day. Ana was enchanted and I too felt a bit dazed by the beauty of it all. What a place to come and live! We left Granada behind and climbed over the pass of Suspiro del Moro, the Moor's sigh, where the last Muslim king had turned to weep as he was exiled forever from his beloved city. Little wonder.

Pedro and Maria had invited us to stay the night and late in the evening we turned into the valley for Ana's first view of our new home. In the light of the setting sun the fields along the road seemed even more beautiful than I had imagined. Ana seemed pleased with it all and I pointed things out to her proudly as we passed. Olives, oranges, lemons . . . cabbages . . . potatoes . . .

We climbed up over the cliffs of the gorge and into the valley.

'There it is!'

You get a brief glimpse of El Valero just as you enter the valley, before it disappears again behind a great curtain of rock.

'Where?'

'Over there, you see? Up on the rock over the other side of the river.'

'That?'

'What do you mean "that"?'

'Precisely that – that.'

'Well "that" is it. El Valero. What do you think?'

'I don't think at all from this distance. I'll reserve judgement till we get a little nearer.'

We drove on into the valley and stopped at a nearer vantage point. 'Well, I think it really looks rather nice.'

I looked at Ana in amazement and delight. She is not generally given to such outbursts of enthusiasm.

16

We drove on a bit and parked the car where the road ran out. From here on we had to walk. 'Piggeries?' she asked. It was undoubtedly a question.

'What?'

'The piggeries?' she asked again.

'What piggeries? There's no piggeries here!'

'You told me that from the road to El Valero was just as far as the piggeries.'

'Did I?'

The light was failing and I knew there was a long and rather tricky walk across the valley to get to the farm. We set off along the path down the hill, navigating a patch of bog where the way forded a stream, and then through a thicket of huge eucalyptus, sweet-smelling and whispering in the evening breeze, and ringing with birdsong. We emerged on the bank of the river. It tumbled full and clear down a steep bed of stones, crashing and roaring over the falls of smooth rocks and gliding in and out of the stiller pools.

I smiled and squeezed Ana's hand as we set out eagerly across the pack-bridge, excited at the prospect of our first view together of our new home.

An hour and a half later it was growing steadily darker and we were thrashing about in a bramble patch up to our ankles in wet black mud. Spanish brambles are more vicious than English ones. Each thorn is a curved barb, and once they've got you they don't much like to let you go.

'I don't know how you had the nerve to say it was only as far as the piggeries.' The matter was clearly preying on Ana's mind.

'Distances can be very deceptive in this sort of terrain,' I said pompously, while slithering about in the mud and dangling rather inelegantly by one ear from a bramble bush. 'But I can't imagine what has happened. I only bought this farm a few days ago and now I can't even find it.'

17

'That is most unlike you.'

I ignored the remark and peered on into the undergrowth. 'This looks like the way I took last time, but it's got a bit over-grown. Let's go back to the big oleander and try the other way.'

At last we burst through a wicked clump of pampas grass in the enveloping darkness, and Ana spotted the pale dust of a path leading through clear ground.

'That's it. I knew it was here somewhere.'

And it was. As we puffed up the path with its rocky steps that had so delighted me when I first saw the place, I turned to Ana triumphantly and grinned at her in the dark. It was a warm night, the breeze scented with unfamiliar blooms, and as we trudged uphill a building loomed above us in the darkness.

The scent of flowers gave way to that of dung and goats. 'This is the house,' I announced, indicating the murky outline with my arm, but Ana's reply was drowned out by the yelping and snarling of the dogs. A door burst open and an ogreish voice cursed into the night.

'Our host,' I explained.

~

The door slammed shut again as we approached. I knocked and waited. The dogs growled and snarled around our knees. Once more the door opened and there stood Romero, with tiny Maria tucked behind his bulk. 'Welcome,' he beamed.

'This is my wife, Ana.'

'Good-looking wife,' said Romero, looking her up and down with a lecherous glint.

'How young you are and how lovely!' enthused Maria, kissing her. 'Come in, come in.'

We entered the room. Romero dealt a deft boot to the dogs sniffing our bags and closed the door behind us.

The sitting room at El Valero was small and square and all whitewashed but for the shiny cement floor. It contained a black plastic sofa facing two wooden chairs and a round table with a television. By way of decoration there was a plastic doll's cutlery set hanging on one wall and a picture of Christ cut from a magazine on another. That was it – and there wasn't a speck of dust. A bare bulb hung in the middle, feebly illuminating the scene.

We were ushered to the sofa. 'No, no!' I protested in my rather stilted Spanish. 'We cannot sit on the only comfortable chair; we must sit on the hard wood.'

'Alright,' said Romero and slumped down onto the sofa, the better to leer at Ana. Ana got up and ratched about in her bag, pulling out an expensive tin of shortbread biscuits and handing it to Maria. Maria looked baffled and handed it to Romero. We all looked at one another in acute embarrassment, except for Romero who was busy prising the lid off the tin. He pulled out a biscuit, considered it and bit off a corner.

'Arrgh! I can't eat that. Tastes of cheese!'

'They're very popular in England, we thought you'd like them.'

'No, we don't.' Romero grinned amiably.

Maria took the tin and put it in a dark store-room nearby. They would put a nice finish on the pigs, those Harrods tartan-tinned Highland Shortbreads.

We sat in silence for a bit, looking at each other.

Maria was the first to crack. 'Welcome to our humble home,' she said. 'It's very poor and very dirty but we're very poor people so what can we do?' She spread her hands and looked mournful.

'No, no, it's wonderful, beautiful – and immaculately clean.' I nodded at Ana, indicating that she should agree. She smiled at Maria.

'We got lost, couldn't find the way across the valley,' I said to Romero, hoping that Ana would continue the conversation I had started so considerately for her about the cleanliness – or other-wise – of houses.

'Of course you did. You didn't know the way,' replied Romero, showing little sympathy and not much inclination to continue this line of conversation.

More silence. I coughed and pinched my leg, then grinned at everyone in turn. Romero grunted and lumbered over to the television and turned it on. The light bulb dimmed. A raucous hissing filled the room and something akin to the sound of massed frogs croaking in a distant pool. Eventually a blizzard appeared on the screen with shadows moving simultaneously up and down and from side to side. Romero moved to one side so we could all watch the screen and raised his head quizzically, inviting our admiration.

'It's a fine television,' I offered hastily. 'Incredible that you can have a television all the way out here. Hah! The wonders of the twentieth century!' But nobody was listening to me; they were all engrossed by the programme – whatever on earth it was.

Romero returned to the sofa and we watched the indecipher-able nonsense on the screen for five minutes or so. I've known some long five minutes in my time but this outlasted them all. Then Romero got up and flicked a switch to change the channel. Another blizzard, more shadows accompanied by distant batra-chian croakings, indefinably different. We all settled down to watch this new extravaganza.

Another five long minutes and Romero had had enough of the second programme, so he got up and switched over again.

'Marvellous,' I said. 'Absolutely marvellous. Tell me, how many programmes can you get on that incredible apparatus?'

'Oh, just the two,' he said deprecatingly. 'This is the first one again.'

So there we sat, the four of us, captivated by whatever scene was unravelling before us, occasionally nodding or grinning at

20

one another in approval, until finally Romero got up and switched the wretched thing off.

'Well, that's enough of that,' I grinned. 'I'm not saying that I don't enjoy TV . . . but really it's no substitute for the – er – for the sweet milk of good conversation . . . is it?'

A thick silence ensued. I felt like a dead pig in a tea-room. I pinched my leg again. I enjoy the sound of my own voice, but this was getting too much even for my thick skin.

'Well, er . . . how does it feel to be going to live in the *cortijo* near the town? It'll be very nice for you, I'm sure.'

'It's a nightmare,' wailed Maria. 'A death. We belong here in our beloved Valero. We are happy here. But we had to sell it and you bought it for less than nothing. We are poor people and now we are poorer – what can we do?' And she spread her hands in that gesture of hers that indicated despair. All this she spoke with a warm and engaging smile.

'Oh dear, I don't want to drive you from your home. We're not going to be moving in for a while. You can stay here all summer. No, for heaven's sake, you can stay as long as . . . ' A fierce cough from Ana drowned the rest.

We resumed the silence, Romero staring fixedly at Ana, until I was spurred into a fresh conversational gambit by a strong smell wafting through the window on the stiff breeze.

'Goats! Got goats here, have you?'

'Yes, goats.'

'They've got goats here, Ana.'

'How interesting.'

'Would you like a glass of milk?' asked Maria.

'Oh please,' we chorused, desperate for some event, some ritual to break the deadlock.

Pedro and Maria both leaped up and shot outside with a saucepan and a torch, slamming the door after them. Ana and I looked at each other in silence for a minute.

'It's going to be goat's milk,' whispered Ana. For some reason, she didn't want to be caught talking while our hosts were out of the room. 'They're going to milk a goat and give us the milk in a glass as if it came from a bottle.'

Maria and Pedro, however, had no such pretensions. Below us we heard a thumping and scuffling, a dark oath and the fart of a goat: then the metallic hiss as the two thin streams of milk spurted into the saucepan. Soon, but not too soon, for I think they too were trying to string the thing out as long as they could, our hosts returned with a saucepanful of white foam.

'Ah – milk,' I said fatuously. 'Would it perhaps be goat's milk?'

'Of course. Now we must boil it.'

Maria took a camping stove and placed the saucepan on it. We all gathered round to watch.

'They're boiling the milk, Ana.'

'Look, apart from the fact that I can see they're boiling the milk, I happen to have studied Spanish for several years. I can more or less catch the drift of what's going on.'

Maria explained that the milk had to be brought to the boil three times before it could be drunk. 'Malta fever.'

This entertainment spun things out for a good twenty minutes, then we drank the horrible stuff. Romero stretched and yawned. I found myself talking again.

'Well, it's been a truly wonderful evening but . . . well, we're so tired we can hardly think straight. Time for bed, I think.'

Everybody agreed enthusiastically. Down the hill, beneath the pomegranate tree, Ana and I cleaned our teeth with the water that dribbled into the drum. It was a clear night with a sliver of bright moon lighting the rivers below us. The pines on the hill opposite were roaring in a high wind.

'Lord in heaven,' hissed Ana in the dark. 'How long are we staying here?'

'Five days, it was supposed to be.'

'Well, I don't think I can stand another evening like that. I suppose you enjoyed it because it was "the real thing"?'

'Enjoyed might be too strong a word. Perhaps we'd better go to town for the next few nights. I'll make some excuse.'

That night the wind rose still higher. It roared through the open bedroom window and blew a chair over. On the chair were Ana's clothes and her glass of water.

~

I had worried that the business of the wind and the chair might have been the end of our whole Andalucian escapade – that is if we hadn't spent our every last bean buying the place and thus burned our boats. But no.

'I think it's wonderful,' said Ana. 'Though I do have certain reservations.'

'And what, pray, might they be?'

She then read to me from a long list of reservations she had prepared. It included recommendations regarding the road, the access, the water – which had not impressed her in its existing state despite the four-piece bathroom suite – and a number of other quibbles too petty to relate.

'Very well,' I muttered absently. 'I'll get all that seen to.'

A SUMMER APPRENTICESHIP

BACK IN ENGLAND WE HAD TO SPLICE ALL THE FRAYING ENDS
of the existence we were about to abandon. In practical terms
this meant clearing our farm cottage and working out the last
few months of our various jobs.

This was a much easier task for me as I had been leading a
more or less itinerant life for the last few years. Most years, I
would disappear abroad for two or three months to help
research a travel guide – I had been sent to China and Turkey,
as well as Spain. Between times, I made a bit of money strum-
ming a guitar in a Russian restaurant in London, and shearing
and looking after sheep on the local farms. Then each Spring
and Autumn, when the coffers got low, I would take off to
Sweden for a few weeks, pursuing more lucrative shearing con-
tracts.

Ana, however, had deeper roots to ease up – literally so, as she
had been running a small horticultural business and needed to
search around for someone to manage it in her stead. There was

also a great deal of paperwork to gather – most importantly the sheaves of obscure documents that were needed for permission to take Ana's beloved familiar, a black labrador-cross known as Beaune, and a few of her treasured plants along with us.

All this we reckoned would take nine months. Just time enough to prepare our relatives and friends for the fact that we would no longer be living amongst them. After six months, however, I found I could wait no longer and, under the thin pretence of learning from the incumbent how to run the farm, I took a cheap flight to Spain to see if El Valero was really there.

~

It was August, a punishingly hot month that year, and, arriving on the bus at Órgiva, I picked my way out of town along an almost dry riverbed. I had a small bag – you don't need much in summer in Andalucía – and, perhaps a little less practically, a guitar in a case.

Towards noon I caught sight of the terraces of El Valero spreading above the riverbed. The farm looked wonderful – and this was the worst time to see it. In the middle of the day the August sun bakes all colour from the landscape. What appear in the slanting rays of morning and evening as misty hills, with clefts and pinnacles of glowing rock, reveal themselves as shadowless wastes of scrub and thorn. Best to ignore the evidence of one's eyes and enjoy only the impressions at either end of the day.

I made a meal out of crossing the river below the farm, drenching myself from head to foot in cool water before climbing towards the house to find Romero. I had written to him, telling him I wanted to spend a month on the farm learning whatever he could teach me about it, and I supposed that his daughter had read the letter for him, for few country people over fifty here have an inkling about their written language.

25

As I climbed across the last terrace where the horses were tethered short in the shade of olive trees, I heard a familiar voice
croaking out a song from the house. There was Romero sitting
on his terrace, throwing stale bread to the dogs in the dust. He
got up and lumbered towards me with a big grin. 'You've come –
and what's this? We shall have music. *Estupendo.*'

'It's good to be here, Pedro,' I panted, wiping away the sweat
that drenched my face.

'It's good that you've come. My people have left to live in town
and it gets lonely up here, though of course I have the beasts –
and there's always God. And then we have the rivers and the
mountains – hah, this is indeed paradise – I shall never leave.
Come on in, I'm just making lunch.'

We ducked our heads and passed through a doorway into the
gloom. It was cooler in the tiny dark room, despite a fire blazing
on the hearthstone. The air outside was simmering around forty
degrees as we pulled two low chairs up to the flames. I watched
as Pedro dazzled me with his artistry in the preparation of his
staple fare, *papas a lo pobre* – 'poor man's potatoes'.

First he put a deep frying-pan, hideously greasy and blackened,
onto a tripod over the flames and into it poured what I judged
to be two coffee-cupfuls (after-dinner size) of olive oil. Then
with his pocket knife he hacked up a couple of onions, without
being too delicate in the matter of peeling them. As they fizzled
gladly in the oil, he pulled to pieces a whole head of garlic and
tossed the lot into the pan.

'Don't you peel the cloves?' I asked.

'Lord no! If you don't peel them they don't burn, and they keep
their flavour better. Less work too.'

He's right as a matter of fact.

He then took a bucket in which were potatoes hygienically
swimming in water; these he had peeled. Squatting over the fire,
sweat pouring from his huge body, he chopped them roughly –

26

great coarse chips, straight into the spitting oil. When the pan was brimful he stirred it about a bit with a stick and added some twigs to the fire for a better blaze. In a basket hanging from a pole were green and red peppers. Taking five or six small ones, he again tossed them in whole.

'Right, that can look after itself for a bit now,' said Pedro, giving it a quick stir, and proceeded to the laying of the table. A wobbly wooden cable drum stood on the terrace. Upon this he placed an old fish-tin which he filled with a huge fistful of olives and a dozen pickled chilli peppers. From a paper sack he took a round loaf of bread like a river-stone and cut it into quarters, returning two to the sack. Then he put two bent forks and two tumblers on the table and went to check the main dish. I sat down and poured wine from the plastic bottle and ate an olive – pickled with lots of garlic, lots of salt and a little less of thyme, lavender and heaven knows what else. A swig of the thick brown wine washed it down.

Gazing absently past the slobbering dogs and down the steep hill, I watched the two rivers curl from the gorge. The hills to the south were almost invisible in the haze of the heat. Another slug of wine and a deep, deep sigh. This was about to be one of those unforgettable meals.

Pedro emerged grinning with the sizzling pan which he plonked onto a tile carefully placed to prevent it staining the cable drum. Then he fetched a huge greasy ham, cut two enormous fatty wedges, and put it back on a hook on a beam. He then sat down on the step, took a swig of wine, and sighed with contentment.

I jabbed into the pan with my fork, gnawed on my ham, gulped my brown wine and chatted to my amiable host. The food was delicious. I did a lot of the cooking that month and it was almost always *papas a lo pobre*, which Pedro favoured for breakfast, lunch and supper, each time with the statutory two glasses of wine. But I never managed quite the same effect with the dish as Pedro achieved.

'You've bought paradise,' he sighed. 'And for nothing. It was a gift. Here you have the finest air and water in the world. I've been around a bit,' and he indicated various spots in the surrounding hills, all visible from the house, 'but I've never found anywhere like this.'

'If you love it like you say you do, Pedro, why did you sell it?'

'My people. My people don't like it here. If it weren't for my people I'd stay here for ever. Here there's the best of everything in the world. There's rich soil – it'll give you the best vegetables you'll ever eat; there's fruit drooping on the trees, sweet water from the spring, and all this glorious fresh air.'

We screwed up our eyes and looked out through the shimmering air onto fields baked by the ferocious sun.

'Nobody will bother you out here; you won't have to worry about the bad milk of the town.'

'The what?' I asked.

'The people of the town, they're rotten right through – not to be trusted, screw you soon as look at you. Nothing, let me tell you, Cristóbal, is as important as being honest and straightforward and treating people right . . . but what do they care? You just be careful of them. Play some guitar.'

I needed no more asking. I took the guitar from its case, tuned it, and pottered into a flamenco piece. Pedro rocked back on his chair, listening with half-closed eyes, then started clapping and singing quietly. He sang badly, disjointed couplets delivered in a cracked groan of a voice, and the guitar-playing was all out of time and with the wrong chords. But we enjoyed it.

Pedro was the first to break off. He hauled himself to his feet, picked up the hunks of stale bread and ham fat from his plate and flung them at the creatures surrounding the table. The meal had come to a close.

'It's too hot to walk with the beasts,' he muttered. 'I'm going to sleep.'

I slept too, or tried to sleep, on a mattress on the floor of the big house, but the flies kept me awake. They were everywhere. I swatted at them and cussed and tossed and turned and all to no avail. I must have slept eventually, though, because I awoke in a boiling sweat to the sound of Pedro's voice ringing round the hills. I hauled my sopping body from beneath the thin sheet and blinked into the blinding light. Seven o'clock, the afternoon gone, but now not only was the sun burning fiercely from high in the sky, but all the hills and rocks were giving back as good as they had got and radiating heat vengefully back into the air. The air, sandwiched between its tormentors, had given up and lay draped over the valley like a rag.

Accustoming my eyes to the glare, I leaned over the terrace and spotted Pedro sitting motionless on his horse down by the river, surrounded by his little group of acolytes. He was singing.

Somewhere in the valley a frog was singing
Polish up my fine crystal glasses . . .

∽

A couple of terraces below the house was to be found one of the miracles of El Valero, a torrent of water that rushed out from a rock and tumbled into a little pool below. I sat in the pool and poured bucketful after bucketful over my head and body. There was a soapdish and a bottle of shampoo and towels and some washing hanging from a wire strung between two acacia trees. Without needing to put shoes or clothes on, I could take just five paces and pick oranges, mandarins, figs or grapes, fresh from the trees. I cooled them in the waterfall and stuffed myself.

From this vantage point I could see a farm in the shade on the west side of the valley. It was a low white building half-buried in

29

surrounding clouds of olive trees. There lived Bernardo and
Isabel and their children, a Dutch family fled from Rotterdam to
farm olives and a few goats. That evening I went to introduce
myself to valley society.

A couple of flimsy poles spanned the river and led to the foot
of the steep path that wound up the hill to the Dutch couple's
farm. As I stumbled across the stony lower terraces, an improbable procession emerged from the shrubbery of the terrace
above. The motive force was a team of several goats, a mule and
a sheep, all harnessed by the forefoot and connected by long
ropes to a sort of human maypole: a large amiable-looking man
who hadn't shaved that day, nor the day before, clad in T-shirt,
floral Bermuda shorts and Wellington boots. Two children
were running up the grassy slope behind him, each swinging a
brightly coloured plastic bucket. The whole scene was oddly
reminiscent of a television advertisement for breakfast cereal.

Suddenly they spied me. 'Whooa!' roared Bernardo, for it was
he. The mule stopped, two goats passed it on the left, one passed
between its legs, and the sheep darted down a bank on the right.

I climbed up to greet him.

'You must be the lunatic who's bought El Valero. We've heard
about you,' he said with a chuckle, attempting to hold out his
right hand but failing. 'Welcome to the valley. Wait while I put
these creatures away and I can greet you properly.'

He set patiently about untangling the chaos of ropes and began
distributing his animals among their various night quarters. 'So,
are you going to come and live here, or just stay here for the
summer holidays?' he asked, leading me to the terrace where
Isabel, his wife, was already laying out some tapas.

'We're going to live here and try and farm the place.'

'Good. I hate to see more land abandoned. Wine for our new
neighbour. We'll drink, if one needs any excuse to drink wine, to
new life in the valley.'

30

Bernardo and Isabel were certainly doing their bit for new life in the valley. They had moved here five years before with their young son Fabian; a daughter, Maite, a sweet-faced child with long tresses of auburn hair, was born shortly after they arrived, and unless I was mistaken Isabel would be 'giving light', as the Spanish put it, again within a month or two. They had bought their farm derelict and abandoned and, with ferocious hard work and the dreamy enthusiasm which city people bring to country living, were turning it little by little into a working farm and a pleasure garden for the children.

There was much to talk about as we drank copious quantities of wine, the same brown stuff Pedro and I had been drinking over the river: *costa* as they call it, in deference to its being grown on the slopes above the coast. I felt relaxed and easy with these people who, with their big booming laughs and infectious good nature, filled the empty space in the valley they had come to occupy.

They told me how pleased Romero was to sell the place and I began to put them right, explaining how he was forever moaning about how much he loved the place and hated to be parted from it – and 'especially for the misery of money I paid him.'

Bernardo looked in danger of choking on his wine. 'He and his people have been desperate to sell that place for years,' he said, 'and they couldn't get to town quick enough. He was about to give it to Domingo for a million – then you came along and gave him five. He must have thought you fell off a Christmas tree! I mean who the hell was going to buy a place that has no access, no running water, no electricity – and that huge patch of land to work? I must say I think it very bold of you to have bought it. Or maybe you are a complete lunatic?'

'I'm at least half-lunatic,' I volunteered. 'But we'll manage somehow. It's an exciting challenge, and anyway, it beats being an insurance clerk working in an office.'

31

'Yes, but you don't look to me like an insurance clerk.'

'No, but I might have been . . .' and I recalled with a shudder the six months I'd once spent in an office.

'Well, it's good to have you here, though we'll miss Pedro and Maria,' said Isabel. 'Maria used to spend a lot of time over here with me, pouring her heart out while we did the washing together. She's nice.'

'And Pedro,' I added. 'I love the way he sings in the valley all alone except for his beasts. He's a natural.'

'He's a natural bad character,' said Isabel, laughing. 'A likeable rogue, you could say, but there's a darker side to him. I'd hate to imagine all his wife has had to put up with.'

'He's always been a very good neighbour to us,' countered Bernardo. 'He's helped me out when I've had a problem no end of times, generous with his time and always good for a laugh. Mind you, I've helped him out, too. We've done a lot of work together. I cleaned the whole of his *acequia* – his water channels – with him this spring. Well, I cleaned it with Maria actually, while he walked with his beasts.'

'It makes me sick the way that lazy swine just sits on his horse "walking with the beasts" all day,' said Isabel.

'Lazy?' I was beginning to feel a little uncomfortable at the consensus forming about my new mentor. 'That man is strong as an ox and works like no one I've ever seen,' I said.

'He's good at putting on a show,' replied Isabel. 'But that'll be for your benefit. He likes to make the right impression. He's got a bad reputation in the valley, and it's justified. I've had a lot of trouble with him.'

'What sort of trouble?'

'He comes round here a lot when Bernardo's out. Says he's desperate to make love to me and if I don't let him he'll shoot himself, and the swine always carries his shotgun with him. "You'll have my blood on your hands!" he says. Well, I tell you I don't fancy him much – he's so old and fat and ugly – and I tell him that, too. So off he goes in a temper, and when he gets round the corner he fires his gun. Of course I rush out to see if he's really shot himself, and when I get round the corner there he is with a big grin on his face. I can't help laughing at it, but it's no joke really because he's so damn big.'

'At least he's slow, though,' said Bernardo, quietly. 'His legs are bad so it wouldn't be too difficult to get away. Anyway we're none of us quite as good as we'd like to be. More wine?'

I worked my way drunkenly home, down the path to the river, in the early hours of the morning. It was a hot night, lit only by the stars and, as a reward for not tumbling all of the way down the steep descent, I treated myself to an hour flat on my back on a warm rock in the middle of the river. The nearest street-lighting was far away, so no dull glow marred the perfect blackness of the night sky, and more stars than I had ever seen glowed and winked. I saw literally dozens of shooting stars.

It must have been the Perseids: mid-August is usually the time for this shower of meteors to pass. But I didn't know about such things then and, anyway, my mind was too occupied with everything I'd heard to think of astronomy. 'It must always be like this on summer nights,' I thought fancifully as I dripped a crooked trail of water up towards the house.

33

A routine soon began to establish itself on the farm. In the morning Pedro and I would tour the terraces and collect the figs that had fallen from the trees in the night. We gathered them in buckets, soft and deep purple and squashy, and took them up to the pigs who lived in a pen at the end of the house. In the pen thcy had a mud pool, a dust-bath and a cool corner shaded by a thick roof, where they panted away the heat of the day. Pigs love figs and they would squabble and bounce about with glee as we emptied about half a hundredweight of the luscious fruit into their stone troughs. Everyone around here keeps pigs, fattening them through the year and killing them, at the traditional *matanzas*, in the fly-free days of winter.

One day Pedro returned from an expedition outside the valley, his horse laden with huge green cannonballs. Water-melon. 'So the pigs don't get bored with the figs,' he explained, cutting each melon into four and tossing them at the ecstatic creatures. 'They're giving them away in the *vega* now, before they plough the rest of the crop in.'

After fig-picking we would cut maize with sickles. The fields below the river were bright with a crop of forage maize, the brightest of the greens at this time of year. We gathered great handfuls of it and severed it at ground level with a curved pull of the sickle.

'Hold it like this, man, or you'll give yourself a nasty cut. You must treat the sickle with great respect.'

Having cut bundles far too heavy for a man to carry, we would hoist them onto our shoulders and trudge bent double up the hill to dump them in the troughs in the various buildings that served as stabling for the cows.

34

We would get these jobs out of the way before the sun touched the fields. Then I would prepare the *papas a lo pobre* or just a couple of thick slices of ham, bread and wine. 'Strong food!' roared Pedro with a manly guffaw. 'Eat strong food!'

Strong food in these parts is chickens' heads, ham fat, pig's blood pudding, raw peppers and garlic, *chumbos* (prickly pear), stale bread and wine. A great deal of manly merit accrues from the eating of strong food and the merit increases the earlier it is taken in the day. Thus a man who can stomach a burnt chicken's head and a hot pepper with a hunk of stale country bread and wash it down with a couple of glasses of *costa* – and do so with relish at breakfast – is a man to be reckoned with.

This was Pedro's preferred diet. He offered me a chicken's head one morning, a ghastly-looking burnt thing with charred feathers on it that he had taken from the fire, waving it under my nose with a grin.

'Strong food for the guest of honour!'

When I demurred, he popped it into his own mouth and crunched it up, a glow of satisfaction suffusing his broad features. In the end I forced myself to submit to such staples for breakfast. It seemed somehow inappropriate to puddle about with cornflakes and milk while others were quite properly devouring more masculine stuff.

After breakfast I would wash the plates, glasses and cutlery on a log of wood by the oil-drum beneath the pomegranate tree. Pedro showed me how it should be done and we were none too fastidious about the quality of the work, except that we always placed a cloth over the crockery laid out to dry, to keep the flies off. After breakfast I was free to entertain myself as I would, while Pedro sat on his horse in the river 'walking the beasts'.

One day I followed the hose from where it dribbled in the drum to its source. Down the hill and up the Cádiar river, snaking in and out of eroded cliffs and swinging across steep drops, it passed a ruined house, no more than a pile of stones, on the boundary of the property, then turned into a deep dead canyon. Nothing grew there on the parched earth but cracked thorns and sinister creepers: capers, as I discovered later. The rocks were coated in a white scale and a deathly sort of silence reigned. High in a barren cleft was a pool; the water dribbled from it through a slimy plastic pipe into a rusty oil-drum. At the bottom of the drum was a hole, and stuffed through the hole, with a bung of rags and string, was the source of the El Valero water supply.

I had for some time puzzled over the fact of the water supply reaching only to below the house, and the well-appointed bathroom had also remained something of a mystery. It was all properly plumbed in – lavatory, bidet, shower and basin – and a copper pipe led through the roof to an oil-drum that was so rusty that it no longer had any discernible form.

Eventually I raised the subject with Pedro.

'The water used to reach the roof and fill that drum, but it doesn't go that high any more.'

He wouldn't expand on that.

'We used to light a fire under the oil-drum and that way we had hot water. It was wonderful.'

~

During the hours when Pedro couldn't think of any work for me to do about the farm, I would go for walks, explore the farm and imagine living here, an idea that still seemed very far from reality. Or I would visit people or sometimes walk into town, an hour and a half away.

This amazed Pedro.

'What on earth do you want to go to the town for? Eating and drinking? Why, we have all the food and drink we could desire right here, and it costs nothing. It's better too – here you know what you're eating, but Lord knows what sort of filth those thieves from the town will be giving you – and then taking your money . . .

'Watching passers-by on their evening promenade? Now look here, Cristóbal' – and here he adopted a tone of great moment – 'You listen here. You are a married man and have a very fine and attractive wife. I am but a simple man, but one thing I can tell you from the bottom of my heart is that you must have respect for your woman. Bad behaviour with other women is a monstrous and terrible vice and brings with it only misery for everyone. You listen to my words because this is really important.'

He thumped his stick on the ground to emphasise the gravity of what he said and looked at me with deep concern.

'Look, I only said that I liked to admire passers-by. I didn't say I would go to bed with them.'

He raised his eyes to heaven in anguish at the very suggestion of such an idea.

'You too, Pedro, have a delightful family and a very fine wife.'

'She's alright,' he grinned. 'Bit dry if you know what I mean.'

'Pedro!' I remonstrated, using the same lugubrious tone of concern that he had used on me. 'Pedro, one does not describe one's woman as "dry".'

'Bah!' he spat.

BRIDGE BUILDING

'WE'RE GOING TO TOWN FOR LUNCH AT THE NEW *CORTIJO*,'
Pedro announced one morning. 'You can ride the other horse.'

I hesitated. It was a while since I'd ridden a horse and I wasn't
sure if I could remember how it was done. Pedro dismissed such
piffling worries. Anyway, he added, he would be leading me.

We gathered food for the beasts, who would remain all day in
their stables, and loaded the panniers on Pedro's horse with a
couple of hundredweight of pot-plants along with odd sticks and
bits of wire, twisted and lashed into arcane forms. When the
horse was fully laden, Pedro neatly swung his enormous bulk off
his mounting-stone onto the top of the load. The horse raised its
eyebrows. I sat on the straw and canvas pack-saddle on the lesser
horse while Pedro held a rope from its head-collar.

'Can't I have some reins, something to hold on to?'

'Hell no! If you hold the reins that horse will take off like a
thunderbolt and kill you good and dead. You've really got to

know how to ride to hold the reins on that horse. Hold on to the saddle.'

I shrugged, resigned, but not altogether sure what to do with those parts of my body that were not occupied with the business of staying on the horse.

'What's it called?'

'Brown.'

'Brown?'

'Brown. It's a brown horse,' said Pedro absently.

One of the dogs was called Brown too; it was a brown dog.

'Yee-haa Brown!!' I cried gaily as we lurched off, the dogs weaving amongst our feet. The horse and its canine namesake looked at me quizzically.

We wound down the path through the oranges and almonds and out into the riverbed where we scuffed among the hot rocks and splashed through the river. The sun blazed down on us from a cloudless sky. In euphoric mood I found myself musing on the idea of waiting in the cold drizzle of an early morning railway-station with hundreds of other besuited businessmen, waiting for the daily ride to the treadmill. 'Whatever comes of this decision,' I thought, 'it has to be better than that.'

The horses stepped delicately down the stony river. The still pines that covered the slopes made the air almost suffocating with their resinous scent. Brown and I were both covered with a film of sweat, and a cloud of happy flies kept station around our heads. The view from the river was wonderful and once I'd got the hang of balancing on the horse (which did not seem quite the fiery creature described by his owner) I was able to gaze around me and enjoy the scenery. You can't do this on foot in the river as the head must be constantly bowed to monitor the progress of the feet.

Soon, though, we left the riverbed and passing through a nar-

39

row defile between two walled orange groves our little band stepped out onto the public highway. We would pass through two villages and countless fields full of farmers before reaching town. Now a mounted rider tends to feel a certain superiority over his humbler pedestrian fellows, by virtue of the advantage of height and also a certain arrogance which the horse, or some horses at any rate, bestow upon their rider. If, however, you are a fully grown man and you are being led on a horse, the effect is considerably diminished. You feel in fact like a prisoner of war, the scurvy dreg of some vanquished foe.

This feeling swamped me the first time one of the toilers in the fields straightened up and turned to watch us go by, our sorry procession of a man, two horses, four scrofulous curs, a thousand flies and a prisoner. How could I assume some kind of dignity in this humiliating position? Snatches of riding lessons popped helpfully up from the dim recesses of memory; the sort of things you never forget: 'Knees in tight, toes up, heels down, back straight and head held erect in a straight line between the horse's ears, a keen and alert mien in the direction of travel.'

I did all these things, first with my arms folded, then with my hands on my hips, then with one hand on my hip and the other wiping sweat from my brow in the way that I imagined a proper horseman would. I nonchalantly scratched parts of my body but soon ran out of parts to scratch. Shielding my eyes from the sun occupied one arm for a useful period. I tried swatting a few flies from the horse's flanks, which helped a bit with the dignity, but I was fighting a losing battle.

40

It simply cannot be done, the maintaining of the merest speck of self-esteem while being led on a mangy pack-horse along a road lined with one's future neighbours, every one of them a natural horseman. Pedro knew this. In fact I soon realised that he must have planned the whole thing for my humiliation.

He made the most of his ploy, hailing everybody we passed to draw attention to Pedro the Conqueror and that extraordinary helpless bag of a foreigner he'd got himself. I could imagine the talk in the valley all too well. 'Romero has got himself this rich foreigner' – all foreigners are assumed to be rich – 'and he pulls him about on that bony old pack-horse like a sack of beans. Poor chap seems to be infested with some sort of vermin. Never stops scratching.'

I withered and died inwardly a thousand times. Slowly, ambling by the back ways and stopping to visit just about everybody who lived on the route, we headed for town. Pedro was also trying to get rid of a dog. We turned up a track, to a house or a field or a garden, where a man would be working, usually back bent to his vegetables. Pedro would draw up his horse; mine would lurch to a stop. 'Eh, Juan. You want a dog?'

The *campesino* in question would slowly raise himself and turn to face Pedro. 'Romero. Good day.'

Then his gaze would turn towards the pack-horse and its helpless load, and the care-worn country face would wrinkle with bemusement. 'What's this?'

'This is the foreigner who has bought El Valero.'

'Buenos dias, mucho gusto,' I would rabbit, wriggling like a clockwork monkey and hoping in vain to assert myself as a human presence.

'No, I don't want a dog and certainly not that dog.'

'Hell of a good dog. Its mother killed a wolf. Fearless hunter.'

'I don't hunt any more, and besides there are no wolves here.'

'This dog's mother finished off the last one.'

'Even so, I don't want it,' and he bent back to his work. 'Go with God, Romero – and your foreigner.'

We would then at last turn away, Romero reaching up with his walking-stick to pull down the branch of a plum tree for us to

41

guzzle. Then on to the next neighbour for the same discussion about the dog, with almost exactly the same dialogue. Pedro was doing a fine job of presenting me to local society.

My feeling of wretchedness grew as we progressed. Finally, as we approached the hill leading up to Órgiva, I wondered how I could wriggle out of being presented to the entire town in the same fashion. We passed a peach tree. Romero reached up with his stick and plucked a few glorious ripe peaches without stopping. He turned in his saddle and with a grin tossed me one. I lunged at it, leaning over from the saddle, and rolled neatly off the horse. Romero politely looked the other way.

'I'll walk for a bit now, Pedro. Arse getting sore.'

'As you wish.' And we set off again, me on foot with the curs at the back of the procession. I wondered that Pedro didn't have me roped up – to stop me getting lost in town.

~

With the pittance I had paid him for El Valero, Pedro had bought a house with a big garden and a stable just on the outskirts of town. It looked like a concrete garage, with its green tin roll-down door. But it had running water and electricity, two modern conveniences that Maria had barely dreamed of before.

We found Maria crouched in a corner of the garage over a fire of sticks. A pot of stew bubbled on a tripod over the flames and peppers roasted in the ashes. We sat on a stone wall beneath the shade of a vine and ate salad and bread, and drank wine while Maria finished the cooking. One small glass of wine and I forgot the whole humiliating business of the ride to town and was brimming with affection for my jolly host. We talked of manly things, of horses and knives and ropes, and crops and watering and hunting and wine. Maria brought dishes of meat and peppers to the table. Pedro loaded my plate with the choicest pieces.

'Eat meat.'

Then he helped himself, while Maria crouched beside him and picked at bits from his plate. This seemed to be their preferred way of eating, she like one of those birds that pick the ticks off the backs of hippopotami.

'Delicious, Maria, a wonderful feast.'

'It is wretched food but we are poor people. We are poorer now that we have sold our beloved Valero – and for the misery of money that you paid – but what could we do?' she smiled.

'Uuoouaargh!' agreed Pedro, working on a huge piece of meat with his molars. 'You've bought paradise – all that air, rich in waters, fine soil, sweet fruits and peace – and for nothing. Eat more meat!' And again my plate was heaped with meat.

Pedro seemed to think it necessary to repeat this mantra to me at least once a day. 'And look what we have now . . . nothing,' he would warm to the theme. 'A dump of a house, a feeble little plot of land, not even enough for the potatoes.'

'Come now, Pedro, it's really very nice – look at all these fruit trees . . . and so convenient for the town, Maria. Life will be so much easier for you here: you won't have to haul water from the river, there are no *acequias* to clean, no steep hills to climb, none of the pains of country life . . . ' I rattled on.

'No scorpions,' offered Maria.

'No what?'

'Scorpions.'

'Are there scorpions?'

'Of course. The place is crawling with scorpions.'

'*Si claro!*' echoed Pedro with a smirk. 'You'll never be short of a scorpion at El Valero. Sometimes in the summer I've had to pour boiling water on the walls to get rid of them all. The walls are running with scorpions.' He scrabbled his fingers graphically across the table-top.

'And snakes,' he continued happily. 'Not too many up at the

43

house, but the valley is alive with them. Thick as my thigh, some of them.'

'Poisonous snakes?'

'No, not so poisonous . . . but dangerous. Chap in the valley had his leg broken by a snake last year.'

'How? How the hell can a snake break your leg?'

'Well, it's mostly when they're on heat. They get aggressive and come steaming at you through the undergrowth, lift their heads up and whop you the most almighty blow. They can knock you clean off your feet.'

Dark shadows clouded my dreams of the sunny farm bright with geraniums and orange blossom. A valley teeming with murderous snakes guarding the entrance to a place of stones and scorpions. Ana was going to love this.

~

It was clear that if we were going to keep at least one foot in the twentieth century when we moved to El Valero, we would need to use a car of some sort. We would also need to improve on the loose arrangement of poles and boulders that currently spanned the river. I had a vague fantasy of leaving El Valero as it was, solitary and untouched by the modern world, and managing with a mule or horses. But pressure was being applied by people whose inclination was more to the practical than the romantic. I had bowed to this pressure before I came in August, promising to see to the building of a road and a new bridge.

Oddly enough I'd never before had the opportunity to build a road, nor a bridge, and I spent a fair few hours wandering about, looking in what I thought was a knowledgeable sort of a way at the possible sites for them. But it was no good. I hadn't a clue about such things and trying to think my way into them just

44

didn't seem to have any effect. I walked over to discuss the matter with Bernardo.

'Domingo is your man,' he advised. 'He knows how to do everything.'

So we went along to see Domingo.

~

As the Rio Trevélez tumbles from its sunless cleft in the mountains and rushes into the broader valley, the first farm it passes is the Cortijo La Colmena. The Melero family have been living there since the time of Domingo's great-grandfather, but they don't own it. As with so many houses and so much land in Andalucía, it is owned by families who live in Madrid or Barcelona and have never even seen the place. Every year Domingo's landlord collects the munificent sum of fifteen hundred pesetas – around five pounds. The tenant pays his own rates, another four thousand pesetas, and is responsible for any repairs or improvements to the place.

For this modest outlay Domingo enjoys the benefit of a house perched up at the end of the valley with a spectacular view of the rivers and mountains; stabling for his handful of sheep, pigs and a donkey; a highly productive vegetable patch, a small vineyard and every sort of fruit tree you can imagine. He also has the fields sloping down to the river, groves of almonds and olives, and rank upon rank of oranges and lemons. All this he cares for seemingly without effort, ambling round the valley on his donkey trailing his feet in the scrub, or lying in the shade of a fruit tree admiring his sheep, or on a really hot summer day in the *acequia* or watering channels, sleeping in its cool water lashed to a root like a boat moored in the reeds.

Domingo lives with his parents, Expira and Domingo – or Old

45

Man Domingo as people call him. Old Man Domingo is a tiny man, leathery with sun and hard work, with a face that cracks constantly into a warm smile.

Bernardo introduced us. We bowed and shook hands. '*Mucho gusto en conocerle* – pleased to meet you,' I said.

Then I turned to Expira, a well-built woman in her fifties who would not very long ago have been a real beauty. She had lovely gay eyes and the smile of someone whose beauty runs right through, like seaside rock.

Domingo himself was sitting on the ground, filing the chain of a monster chainsaw. He greeted me with a friendly grin.

We sat on low chairs around a cable drum. These cable drums are ubiquitous here; they make very good tables. The Sevillana, the electricity-generating company of Andalucía, has a generating station and a storehouse in the valley. So all the surrounding farms are liberally bestowed with the detritus of power generation. Over the years Pedro Romero had built an impressive collection of hawsers, girders, tensioning devices, ceramic insulators, steel rods and cables. 'You can always find some use for such things and if you don't nick it when you can, it won't be there when you need it for something,' he had explained.

Expira carefully placed a sack over their drum, its lively colours showing its provenance as a sugar refinery on the coast, and served us with wine, bread, olives and ham. It was that hour of day . . . although exactly which hour of the day that is, I cannot quite say, as it always seems to be that time. We sat in a cloud of flies – there has to be some flaw in every paradise and flies had clearly been allocated to mine – and talked about the river and the valley and farming.

'So you're going to live at El Valero, are you?' asked Old Man Domingo.

'Yes, we're moving down in the winter.'

'El Valero is a good farm,' he mused. 'Plenty of sun and air and rich in water . . .'

'So they say.'

'The pity is that it's on the wrong side of the river. That river can swell with winter storms and you could be completely cut off for weeks or more. There was a woman died over there not too long ago. Her appendix swelled up: she was in great pain. They tried to get her across the river with the mules, but the current was too strong, knocked the mules over, so she died. Horrible.'

'Yes, and then there was Rafaela,' added Expira. 'You know Rafaela Fernández, the deaf one's daughter – she died in childbirth at El Valero. The river got up and took the bridge away. You'll have to do something about it. It's too dangerous living there with no bridge.'

From here all we could see was a thin red trickle curling between the boulders in the riverbed.

'It's been a dry summer,' continued Old Man Domingo. 'Catastrophic. Hasn't rained a drop since March. It just doesn't rain like it used to do. Even in summer it used to rain, though it just did a lot of damage then, no good at all. I remember one summer a few years ago, along came a cloudburst . . . it was a bright, clear day and nothing but a dribble of water in the river, like now, and then suddenly there was a great rush of water and the river was full of dead pigs and goats and mules. The water actually went over the top of the Seven-Eye bridge down below the town. Yes, it certainly knew how to rain in those days.'

'If it doesn't rain any more then I needn't bother to do anything about the bridge,' I suggested hopefully.

'But you never know what's going to happen in the future. There could be a thunderstorm tomorrow. You can never trust the river. You should build a bridge and a road in and a road out

47

up the back way in case the river takes the bridge.' This was from Domingo, who had put aside his chainsaw and was drawing up a seat by the cable drum.

'Up the back? You mean put a road right up that mountain?!'

'It's not that far. Three or four bends will take you up to the mining road at the top. A good digging machine would do it in a couple of days.'

'Well,' I said. 'Then we'll have to put in a road and a bridge. But a bridge is going to be an expensive and difficult business ...'

'No, no, no, cost you pennies,' he declared. 'Just a few eucalyptus beams thrown across and a couple of piers made with some cement and river stones. You don't want to spend any money building in the river. Whatever you build is bound to get washed away.'

'Right then, some eucalyptus beams ...'

'That's simple enough,' said Domingo. 'Now is the waning of the August moon – just the time for cutting eucalyptus beams. Cut them at any other time, apart perhaps from the waning of the January moon, and they'll rot. Juan Salquero owns that eucalyptus grove down the river there. I'll square it with him and we'll cut them tomorrow. To do the job really well we'll want five fifteen-metre beams.'

Next morning I arrived to find Domingo forty feet up a tree with his chainsaw – no gloves, no ropes, just his usual outfit of ragged sneakers, thin trousers and shirt. He had wedged himself in a fork and was leaning out with his foot hooked round a branch. The huge chainsaw, an ancient and terrible machine, unencumbered by any modern safety devices, was gnawing ferociously away at a thick trunk of poplar that was in the way of the operation.

Domingo really was a phenomenon. When he was around, things that appeared impossible got done as if by magic. In no time at all we, or rather he, had cut down five huge straight-

48

trunked eucalyptus, trimmed them up and taken the bark off them, then covered them with brush so the sun didn't bake them too quickly. There they would lie until winter when we would find some way of hauling them out of the wood to wherever we decided to put the bridge.

I hadn't fancied using the chainsaw myself so I did the trimming with a hand-axe, and the peeling of the bark. We worked away through the morning until Domingo called a halt. 'Come on,' he said, 'Let's go and drink a glass of wine on the terrace. It's too hot out here now.'

So we went up to Domingo's place where Old Man Domingo was sitting on a box not too far from a jug of wine, making baskets out of esparto grass.

'For my niece,' he explained. 'She has a restaurant in Granada. Wins cookery prizes. She likes to have lots of esparto baskets all over the place, goodness knows why! Her customers are all doctors and professors and what have you. She's just round the corner from the university. She says they feel at home with all these things from the country. Me, what do I know?'

The middle of the day was, like every other middle of the day, scorching hot, but up on the Meleros' terrace we were fanned by a gentle breeze and the roof was shaded by a giant eucalyptus. The air shimmered in the valley below us. I could see Pedro and his train of beasts heading up the path from the river for their siesta. From the olive groves on the western slope came the clink of a plough and the sound of Bernardo cursing his mule.

'Beautiful, isn't it?' said Expira. 'We're poor as can be and life is nothing but drudgery and pain, but I love this view.' She smiled as she swatted at a cloud of flies with a dishcloth.

'Yes, beautiful,' I agreed. 'I can hardly believe that we're really going to come and live here.'

'Do you have any children?' she asked.

'No, but we're thinking about it.'

49

'Thinking about it won't do any good. You must have children, you'll be so lonely otherwise all the way over there on your own. The valley needs more children. I need more children. My grandchildren are in Barcelona and I only see them once a year, and this one' – she indicated her son – 'this one doesn't seem to want to get married. You couldn't perhaps find some girl from "over there" for Domingo to marry, could you?'

'I'll see what I can do,' I laughed.

~

I had fulfilled a part of my brief. The new bridge was under way, even to the extent of something practical being done about it – the cutting of the beams. Next, Domingo and I headed off into the Alpujarras in search of a machine-man to build the road.

In the car Domingo explained all there was to be known about machines. There were pits into which the unwary and uninformed could easily drop. There were machine-men who were crooks; there were machine-men who were incompetent; some were too timid and some were too reckless, and some even were unreliable. And then of course there were the machines. Domingo's *bête noire* was the machine with rubber wheels.

'Whatever we end up with, we don't want a machine with rubber wheels. They're no good. Estéban has one with rubbers, and he's a good driver, but he's a crook so we won't go to him.'

'Didn't you say that Estéban was a friend of yours?'

'Yes, he is.'

'But you just said he was a crook.'

'Even crooks need friends, and anyway I like him, crook or no. His machine is old, though, and completely knackered, another reason it'd be no good. You don't want an old machine. You'll pay the same hourly rate but the thing will get tired and won't work as hard as a younger one. And of course you don't want a new machine either, because a man with a new machine will be frightened to scratch the paintwork and he won't push it hard enough.'

My head was spinning with the complexities of the task. We sped back and forth through the mountains, stopping everywhere a machine-man had been spotted. We interviewed dozens of machine-men in bars, or in pyjamas at their doors after midnight, inspecting critically their plant and discussing the merits of various arms, blades, buckets, tracks, wheels, shovels and grabs.

Eventually we settled on Pepe Pilili and his machine. Between Órgiva and Lanjarón is a *tasca*, a thing too humble to be classified as a bar or *venta* – a sort of wayside watering-hole – and beside it is a little *ermita* or wayside chapel, decked in flowers. Long after midnight and a fruitless evening searching for a machine, we pulled up.

'Pepe Pilili lives here. He has a machine,' Domingo announced.

Pepe was there in the bar, cuddling his new baby. Once acquainted, you wouldn't forget Pepe Pilili. He was tall with thick blond hair and cocky as a sparrow.

'No problem, my friend. I'll do your road for you. Start tomorrow evening.'

We celebrated our pact with sangria, a mixture of red wine, lemonade and brandy. You don't get much sangria in the Alpujarras, which made the occasion a particular treat. Then Domingo and I returned home in jubilant mood. On the way Domingo confided to me that Pepe's machine, a JCB, had rubber wheels, that it had been delivered from the factory only the week before, and that Pepe had never actually driven a machine in his life. 'It'll be alright, though,' we assured each other. 'You can't afford to be too fussy in these matters.'

A week later Pepe Pilili turned up with his shiny new machine. To a man like myself, lately come to the business of appraising

51

such apparatus, it looked businesslike – despite its immaculate paintwork and rubber wheels. It splashed across the river, made itself a ramp to get up the sandy bank, devoured a clump of bushes, the last obstacle to arriving on the farm, and there it stood, gleaming in the last rays of the evening sun.

Pedro and his goats shuffled up to give it a critical scrutiny. 'What do you think, Pedro?' I asked. 'Don't you feel a bit sad that the world is about to thrust its grubby arm into El Valero, and cut a road through these timeless terraces?'

'The Host, no! This is the future, man. This is what El Valero needs. I'd have done it years ago if it hadn't been for my people. Pity about the machine, though.'

'What's wrong with the machine?'

'It's got rubber wheels.'

Domingo steered his donkey through the scrub to come and supervise. 'We'll start with that bank there, Pepe. Off you go – and cut in as close to the almond as you can. We want to waste as little good land as possible.'

Pepe launched his machine at the bank indicated by Domingo. I disappeared up to the house to fetch some beer. Coming down I was surprised to see the JCB in an unusual attitude. It was lying on its side at the bottom of the bank. Pepe was scratching his head beside it, Pedro was sniggering, and Domingo was scornfully explaining to Pepe just what he should have done.

'Get it up on its feet again and start the bank from the top this time.'

'How in God's name am I going to get it back on its feet again?'

Pepe's cockiness was more or less unruffled but I could see that he was shaken by what could have been a horrible accident.

'With the arm, of course. That's what the arm's for.'

'I don't know, Domingo – you try.'

'Me? I've never driven a machine.'

Saying which he clambered into the cab and started the engine.

52

As he tried out the controls to see which did what, the machine wriggled about on the ground like one of those one-legged grasshoppers. Then slowly it raised itself on its arm, wobbled about a bit – a clever twitch of the bucket – and bonk, it bounced back onto its rubbers.

'There,' said Domingo, climbing from the cab rather pleased with himself. 'No damage, still works.'

Pepe climbed back in and attacked the bank again rather timidly from the top. The rest of us sat on the grass with our beer and watched. As I looked up from this little earth bank, my eyes scanned the huge expanse of rocky hill that we would have to cut through to get to the old mining road at the top. To be truthful, Pepe and his machine and its wretched rubbers were not the ones for the job.

∾

Next day we headed off in search of another machine-man Domingo knew of – Andreas of Torvizcón. We arrived in the town and were directed to his house, where his wife told us that he was out cutting tracks in the Contraviesa ten kilometres from town. After an hour or so of cruising about on the dusty tracks through the almond groves and vineyards that cloak the hills of the great counterscarp of the Sierra Nevada, we found him.

Domingo hailed him and there followed the usual half-hour of unfathomable conversation which, strain as I might, I couldn't catch a word of. Then the machine-man came over to me and shook hands.

'I'm the man for your job,' he said with a grin. 'Want to see what my machine and I can do?'

'Alright, go ahead.'

He had already hopped onto his bulldozer, no half-arsed dust-pecker on rubbers this one, but a proper machine with tracks.

There followed an astonishing virtuoso performance in which the little red machine, all but invisible in a cloud of sunlit dust, cavorted and pranced on a near vertical hillside. Occasionally I caught a glimpse of Andreas's face, lit up with a grin as he deftly flicked the levers and sent the machine waltzing gracefully backwards up a terrifying slope. In half an hour this dazzling and improbable ballet came to a close and Andreas was hired to put my road in. Tomorrow he would come to walk the land with Domingo and me.

The road was to be finished by November, and Pedro Romero was engaged to be the impartial arbitrator who would check the hours worked daily and resolve any questions that arose over where or how to put the track. Andreas insisted upon this arrangement so there could be no question of foul play: not that there was any question of foul play, but you know what people are like.

MOVING IN WITH PEDRO

IN THE AUTUMN WE BOUGHT AN OLD LANDROVER AND trailer, loaded it with the carefully chosen remnants of our former life and took the ferry for France. For six days we lumbered south through France and Spain, huddled in the cab. Ana, Beaune and I. The Landrover was slow, the load was heavy, and the hills were long, so there was plenty of time for reflection. We stared morosely through the pathetic little wedges of window cleared by the wipers, not saying much.

It had been very grand to say to everyone at home, 'Oh we've bought this farm in the mountains of Granada – you know the kind of thing, no road, no power, no water, no nothing. Oh yes, we thrive on a bit of adventure, not for us the dismal round, that's the way we are!'

And then we found it was actually happening. We had tossed aside all that was comfortable and predictable about our lives and hurled ourselves out into the cold. Anyone passing us on the road might have thought we had the look of refugees forced to leave a beloved homeland, but we weren't so much depressed, just numbed with surprise to find ourselves actually taking part in a script we ourselves had written.

It seemed endless, the long tedious inclines up mountain ranges drained of colour by drought and frost, then the plains at the top, with the chill wind whipping the roadside dust. Then late one afternoon on the fifth day we found ourselves creeping down a long pass with dramatic green-cloaked rock formations on either side. As we descended we seemed to enter a different world. The washed browns of the grass above turned to rolling meadows of deep green, sprinkled with autumn flowers. The sun shone warmer, the sky was blue and we peeled off layer after layer of woolly clothes. Little white farmhouses, bright with flowers, were tucked into shady valleys and everywhere was the cloudy green of olive trees. We were coming down the pass of Despeñaperros and entering Andalucía.

~

At El Valero, the roadbuilders had cleared a wide bare space by the old pomegranate water-butt and there we came to rest. Beaune leapt from the Landrover and set about investigating her new domain. Of course she wouldn't have seen it then as her domain, just another night-stop on a seemingly endless journey. And it must have looked a pretty odd sort of hotel.

'Well, here we are. This is home. Here we lay our bones.' We laughed and walked arm in arm up to the terrace where we sat dangling our legs over the drop below while the sun slipped down behind the hill.

What we needed was a cup of tea. If you're English, or for that matter Chinese, you always need a cup of tea at such moments, even if you're just moving into your new home on the continent.

So we set about gathering the wherewithal for a brew. Nothing that we had brought with us up to the house was suitable for that purpose and I refused adamantly to unload and go back across the river to where we had left the trailer before I had drained my first cup.

We eventually found a bent aluminium pot. The sort of pot you boil up handkerchiefs in. It looked as if a mule had trodden on it. Then we built a fire of twigs, filled the pot with water from the pomegranate-dribbling hose, and suspended it over the flames with some bits of rusty wire. When the water began to smoke – not steam, oddly enough, but smoke – we removed it from the heat and put in some sort of tea-bag we'd located. Then we covered it with a flat stone to mast.

'Cups, cups, cups . . . what shall we do for cups?' But of course! There were some empty tuna-fish tins lying around here and there. I took a couple and went to scrub them in the water-butt.

'Have six minutes elapsed yet?' They had, and we poured the loathsome grey liquid into the tuna tins.

'You didn't wash the cups very well,' said Ana accusingly.

'I did the best I could – they're alright.'

A scum of fish-oil was floating on top of the tea. We sat back and sighed, gazing at the lovely view of rivers and mountains below us, while we sipped what must surely have been the most detestable beverage ever to pass the lips of man.

Nonetheless, we have kept as family treasures the paraphernalia of that first brew and on November 26 each year we celebrate El Valero Day by seeking to surpass in vileness that first momentous cup of tea.

57

Romero came up and watched as we unloaded the Landrover. 'What's this for? What on earth do you do with these?' he asked as he fingered and rubbed all the myriad things that had no place in his simple countryman's armoury.

'It's a thing for slicing eggs . . . an asparagus kettle. That? Oh that's a tea-cosy . . . for keeping tea-pots warm . . . a device for applying rubber rings to the balls of lambs, a pepper-mill, a food-processor . . . a word-processor . . . ' I felt more and more abashed as, with my explanations, I laid bare for him the fripperies of our existence. It seemed somehow wanting when compared with the elemental earthiness of his.

Alpujarran man has no need of such dross. He makes do with what he has got or what he can find for nothing. Give him a plastic fizzy drink bottle and half a hank of baler-twine and he will create an object of delicate beauty that is also functional in that it keeps your water or wine cool – or just below the boil at any rate – in the heat of summer. An old car tyre will become a pair of sandals for irrigating. A bit of bone sees use as a doorstop. The plants that grow on the hillsides furnish just about everything the home needs.

'And what in the name of the Host is that?'

'What?'

'That!'

'It's a bed.'

'But it's made of wood. You can't have a wooden bed!'

'Why ever not?'

'It breeds chinches. Wood breeds chinches.'

'Well, what might chinches be, then?'

'They're the *bichos* that sting and bite you at night. There's enough of them here as it is. You don't want to go encouraging them with a wooden bed!'

I knew we'd never be able to get everything right in Pedro's eyes. We liked the wooden bed, so the wooden bed stayed.

~

'I'm making something to eat,' said Pedro. 'Come and join me.
It's *papas a lo pobre*.'

Ana gave me a look.

'It's really very nice of him: I do think we should accept his
invitation. Thanks Pedro. We'll be down in ten minutes.'

I banged some big nails into the arms and legs of the home-
made wooden bed to cut down on the wobble. The floor of the
room fell steeply away towards the goat-stable below, so I also
stuffed some books and magazines under the feet to level it. Ana
wiped every last speck of dust from the bedroom and then
opened the window wide to let in the fast-moving night air and
the ever present miasma of goat.

Pedro still did his cooking in the lower part of the house. It was
dark and starlit as we walked down the path, and the air was
sweet with jasmine and woodsmoke. There was an electric light-
bulb hanging in the middle of the room but Pedro was much too
frugal to use it. The twig fire blazing beneath the black pot of
potatoes illuminated the scene, aided by a skilfully adapted tuna-
fish tin with old oil floating inside and a rag for a wick. Shadows
and low light danced on Pedro's big body as he crouched over
the fire with his preferred stick, stirring the happy concoction.

'Cristóbal, you lay the table and pour some wine for Ana.'

I set the drum and poured Ana some *costa*. She took the glass,
sat beside the makeshift table and gazed down at the river. It was
a less fine wine than she might perhaps have wished for (Ana
had, after all, named her favourite dog after a particularly delicious wine from Hospices de Beaune) but she sipped it without
a murmur. I had hoped she would station herself by the cook
and chat about recipes or the like, but no, it seemed that Ana was
not quite so sure about Romero as I was.

That first meal was not a success. I did my best to lubricate the
wheels of sociability but the gulf was great. Pedro had decided
on some whim that he couldn't understand a word of what Ana

59

was saying, despite the fact that she was at least as fluent as I was. Ana returned the favour by withdrawing from the conversation and the meal soon degenerated into an embarrassing exchange of grunts and sighs, punctuated by long silences.

'Is he going to cook that for us every night?' Ana whispered as soon as we were alone. 'And how long do you think he intends to stay? He's alright in his way, I suppose, but he's rather an oppressive presence, don't you think?'

'Well, I can't deny it would be nice to be alone,' I had to agree. 'But we have to remember that we are pushing the poor man out of his home and livelihood . . .'

'No we are not. We've bought the place from him and he has a perfectly good home to go to with a wife and family waiting for him.'

'Yes I know, but he loves it here. He says it's his spiritual home.'

I thought it best not to mention the wild offers I had made in the summer about running the place in partnership with Pedro, of how he would have a home with us for as long as he wanted. I was not well versed in the niceties of buying and selling properties and was still working on the assumption that the buyer was taking cruel advantage of the poor oppressed seller, a part Pedro and his family played very well.

'Well, I hope he doesn't make it his home, spiritual or otherwise, for too much longer. It's one thing buying a peasant farm, it's quite another buying the peasant with it.'

I blushed inwardly at the word. Ana has a sharp tongue, though one often frighteningly close to the mark.

'No no, don't worry, he'll be gone soon enough. Anyway I think we have a rare privilege to be living here and benefiting from the knowledge and skill of this noble . . . er, noble . . .'

'Peasant?'

'You know I don't like that word, Ana. I really do think it would be as well not to use it.'

'Alright then, noble what?'

'Son of the . . . no, master of the soil. '

'Pompous fart! He's a peasant, Chris. What's wrong with saying it?'

'Alright, noble peasant.' I choked out the word with difficulty. 'But to get back to what I was saying, there are not many people who are as lucky as we are in being able to get to grips with a foreign culture by actually living in the same house as one of the local . . . '

'Peasants.'

'Yes, one of the local people.'

This conversation was taking place hissed in the darkness by the pomegranate tree with its oil-drum of grubby water. We were cleaning our teeth in it. We decided to leave the washing up for the light of the morning, and retired to bed. Romero had his bed in the next room but one – all of which were connected by doorless doorways. It was a lovely night, with a gentle breeze and a clear sky. We left the window open, as was our custom, and despite the unaccustomed noises slept deep and soundly.

~

I've never been good at getting up early in the morning. The warmth and comfort of a good bed shared with an agreeable companion have always triumphed over the potential excitements of a new day. And this morning, our first in our new Spanish home, was no exception. The delights of my warm careless slumber were, furthermore, compounded by confusion as to what to do with the momentous day that lay ahead. What should one do on the first day of a new life? It would be so easy to make a mess of it. Best perhaps to fudge the issue and stay in bed.

The almost reflex imperative of making my sleeping wife a cup of tea, however, soon asserted itself and I had fully roused myself

61

before I remembered the cup we had shared the evening before. We could breakfast together later, I decided.

Through a frame of dark ivy I could see the low sun brightening the geraniums and roses that lined the path of beaten dust and cow-dung. The sound of animals grunting and burbling rose from the surrounding stables. It all looked worth investigating so I shuffled down to the oil-drum to splash my face with water. As I came back up the track, Pedro was edging his way down, mollusc-fashion, with his bedding piled high on his head and shoulders and dragging in the dust.

'You're not moving out, are you?' I asked, incredulous.

'No no, but you left the window open in your room last night. The night airs will kill you good and dead.'

'Nonsense, man,' I reassured him. 'We've spent all our lives with the bedroom windows open, in colder weather than you've ever known, and we're still alive.'

'That's as may be – over there – but here the breezes of the night are absolutely fatal. I had an uncle who visited someone once and passed the night in a room where the window didn't quite shut properly; no big thing; mind you, just a crack in the casement. Anyway, the next morning he woke up sick as can be, was dead by nightfall, and is now in the glory.'

And he raised his eyes to heaven in that way that people here do whenever the glory comes into the conversation.

'Blimey, Pedro, that was more than just a crack. We had the window open wide all night, and we're alright – well, I think we are. I'll just go and check that Ana's okay.'

'You've had a lucky escape but I'm moving out to the other house. Another night like that and I may not be so lucky. I have to take care, I'm old and feeble but I have no wish to pass to the glory yet.'

I sat on the bed, checking that Ana had not succumbed to the lethal effects of the night breeze. She seemed alright.

'Where's my tea?' she said.

'Do you really want a morning cup of tea?'

She weighed this carefully. 'No, definitely not.'

'I think Pedro is making *papas a lo pobre* and you could wash it down with a couple of glasses of *costa*.'

'I'd rather die.'

'It would appear that you nearly did, me also, and we nearly did for Pedro into the bargain. He says the night wind is absolutely lethal and you should never sleep with the windows open.'

'That man talks more cock than a cartload of hens. Really, I've never heard anything so ridiculous.'

I assumed a pained expression at Ana's choice of language.

'Of course, of course, but you never know.'

Ana got up, Beaune bounded off the bed, and the three of us went outside and watched the morning sun play with the shadows on the hills opposite. From below came the smell of frying potatoes, onions and garlic – strong food.

A notion was forming in my head that the right thing to do on the first morning of our new life would be to climb the hill behind the house and survey our new domain together.

'I can't see why we have to clamber all the way up there to see the farm which is down here,' said Ana.

'Well, for one thing, it's a natural and wholesome human urge to want to get to the top of whatever hill one sees. Without that urge we would scarcely be human . . . would we?'

'That urge, as you put it, is utterly lacking in me.'

'Don't you long to know what's over on the other side of a mountain?'

'In the unlikely event of my curiosity being that strong, I think it would be far more sensible to drive round and see whatever it

63

is as it's meant to be seen,' Ana countered. 'Viewed from its own level ground.'

Bernardo has an interesting comment on this subject. He too used to be possessed by that admirable urge to climb to the peak of whatever prominence he encountered, but living in the mountains changed all that and now he has not the least desire to climb even the humblest hillock. In fifteen years, he admits, he has never even seen the top of his own land, finding more than enough to occupy himself at the bottom of it.

Still, such sentiments lay well ahead of me and I eventually cajoled Ana into the climb by dwelling on the healthy exercise the dog would get from such an expedition.

Beaune raced gleefully into the scrub leaving us to climb slowly up behind her towards a concrete blockhouse perched at the hill's summit. Amazingly enough, this blockhouse once presided over an aerial cableway that fifty years ago transported minerals across the valley, from the Minas del Conjuro ten kilometres to the east, out to the port of Motril thirty kilometres to the southwest.

Once at the top, Ana seemed well pleased with the view. You lose the sound of the rivers up on the heights and a curious silence reigns, punctuated only by the cries of the tutubias and the breezes sighing in the broom. Beaune's fur and our trousers were coated in scent from the bushes of rosemary we had bashed through and the fragrance was made more interesting by the addition of lavender and several varieties of thyme, tinged by the odd clump of evil-smelling rue.

Far below, the clear water of the gently flowing Cádiar river mingled with the darker rushing waters of the Río Trevélez and together crashed and tumbled down the rocky bed to the gorge at El Granadino. In the easternmost of the three triangles made by the joining of the rivers lay El Valero. We sat on a hummock and traced the edge of the land as it fell steeply almost to the water's edge on the south side, and flattened into wide river-fields on the north.

~

Back at the farm, with half the morning still ahead, I bounced across the river in the Landrover to fetch another load of our ridiculous and embarrassing worldly goods from the trailer. It was doubly embarrassing now, for the occupants of the few houses nearby had gathered to pass muttered comments on each item as it emerged.

'That must be their pig-killing table.'

'No! Do they really use things like that over there?'

In fact it was our dining table, a fine piece of joinery that I had once hauled back from an antique shop for Ana's birthday. Interestingly, nobody seemed to want to hazard a guess about my electric sheep-shearing equipment, which was greeted with a puzzled silence.

Chastened by this reception of our possessions, I crept up the river again to unload in front of Pedro, who subjected each and every object to yet more critical commentary. I thanked the unseen powers that had made us leave Ana's collection of china toads and turtles by a roadside in England, when our trailer had proved too heavy to budge.

By the end of the morning I had moved our remaining gear from the trailer and installed it in the house. Ana, with a dust-pan and brush and some jam-jars full of flowers, had made the place into some semblance of a home. As I rumbled up the track with the last load, she was sitting with Pedro, eating lunch.

'Pedro and I have drawn up a list of what we need,' Ana announced. 'Running water, that's the main thing,' asserted Pedro. 'Proper civilised people like you should not be without running water.'

65

I gaped. Since when had he transformed himself into such an advocate of modern living? But Ana was away. 'You must have had running water here once?' she asked Pedro. ' What about the oil-drum on the bathroom roof?'

'Ah, we used to fill that up with buckets from below. The old spring we used would never reach that high. What you must do is buy some hose and run it to one of the springs on the other side of the valley, in the *barranco*. I've been wanting to do that for years but you know how it is: my people, they wouldn't hear of it. They won't part with a penny, my people.'

'That's a hell of a long way to run a hose,' I objected. 'And besides, we don't have any rights to that water.'

'Lord, that doesn't matter!' Pedro scoffed. 'That's lost water, anyone can have it. You'll be alright with that. As for the distance, well, it's less than a thousand metres, and it should be high enough to give you good pressure in the bathroom. It's fine sweet water too, you can drink it. You'll have spring water to drink in your own house and plenty left over for watering. You'll be able to turn the place into a paradise. The first thing is to get a new oil-drum for the bathroom roof. Then Ana will need a cooker – she can't possibly cook like me over this disgusting twig fire. And you'll need a fridge to keep the beer cold.'

'I think he's more or less got the priorities right,' said Ana with a grin.

66   'Water, cooker and fridge; then we'll get some food in and we'll be away. We'll go into town after lunch.'

$$\sim$$

So we went to town in search of an oil-drum and cooker. I couldn't whip up a great deal of enthusiasm for the fridge, as the weather was pretty cool at the end of November, and I've never liked cold beer. I also rather liked the romance of cooking in a dark corner over a twig fire. Ana was adamant, however, so we searched out a gas cooker. Of course there were no oil-drums to be had in town, so we had to buy a big new plastic one. A roll of hose, some sausage and some wine – these last despite Pedro's earnest protestations – completed the day's purchases.

'Why on earth you want to pay good money to buy food beats me,' said Pedro with a pained look when we got back with our purchases. 'The farm is bursting with good food and we have lots of wine. There's a whole clamp of potatoes under a pile of brush-wood by the acacia trees. There's sacks of onions, lots of garlic, peppers and tomatoes still on the plants, and aubergines too, as well as olives and oranges and ham . . . and, *vaya*, there you have it – *papas a lo pobre* . . . Of course, occasionally it is no bad thing to buy a tin of tuna or sardines to add to the potatoes, you know, vary the diet a bit, but this habit of buying all this unnecessary food, it hurts me a lot.'

~

Pedro's insistence that running water in a house was worth some expenditure of energy and money may have been out of charac-ter but he had a point. Ana was certainly convinced, so the next day I set to fixing up some sort of system. I carried the tank up to the saddle of the hill above the house and connected the hose to a more or less round hole that I'd punched and filed in the bottom. Then I rolled the hose down the hill and, with a length of wire and an old bit of rubber tubing, connected it to the bit of copper pipe that stuck out of the bathroom roof. Then with some string, a rag, and a plastic bag, I stuffed up the hole in the bottom of the tank.

After this we gathered every bucket and tub and bottle and drum we could find, and headed in the Landrover down to the river. We filled them all and crept back along the stony riverbed

67

towards the house. A great bounce up the hill by the entrance to the lower fields and we lost half the water at one huge slop. It took us twenty minutes of careful creeping to get back to the tank. What remained was about fifty litres. It didn't look much swilling about at the bottom of a five-hundred-litre tank but it would do to get us started. I ran down to the bathroom and called Ana in to watch as I turned on the tap . . . Nothing, not even a burble, emerged.

'I can't understand it. It's so simple, surely it has to work. There must be some factor I've left out of my calculations.'

'*Abejorros*,' said Pedro from the doorway. 'The pipes are probably full of *abejorros* nests.'

Abejorros are like huge black and blue bees. They wobble clumsily about on hopelessly inadequate but very beautiful blue wings. Opinion differs as to whether they sting or not. They give the impression of being able to deliver a very nasty sting indeed, but as I've never been stung by one myself, I give them the benefit of the doubt. They build their nests in any interesting hole that presents itself, mainly hollow canes, but also in pipes and hoses if they are left idle for long enough. When we disconnected the hose and poked a piece of wire into the copper pipe we found it was stuffed full of dead *abejorros* and their nests.

I scraped out the detritus and reconnected the pipes. Back down to the bathroom, a little disconcertedly this time, as I couldn't help noticing that there hadn't been a drop of water anywhere near the insects. Again I turned on the tap. Again the humiliating silence. Now I know nothing about plumbing, and the world of Johnson couplers, header-tanks and back-pressure is one that I'd rather leave the lid on. But at least one elementary notion had rubbed off on me from school physics: water apparently always runs downhill. This law didn't seem to be holding good here. I looked desperately at Pedro, who was picking his teeth with his knife, leaning on the doorpost.

68

'Air in the pipe.'

'Of course there's air in the pipe, but what can I do about it?'

'Suck the tap.'

'I can't suck the tap. I can't get my head in the bloody sink!'

'Disconnect the shower and suck that.'

So I sucked the shower until my head went red. There was a horrible noise of blubbering and slobbering, a whoof of air, and out came a dribble of brown water.

'Something's happening!' I yelled. The brown dribble stopped. More air hissed out, the pipe snaked about a bit, coughed, then – mercy be! – a clear jet of water shot from the shower-hose.

Jubilation indeed. Running water had finally arrived in the bathroom of El Valero.

'It's not really running water,' cautioned Ana. 'Not if you have to drive all the way down to the river to fetch it.'

'Look, you turn on the tap – water comes out of it. That's running water in my book.'

But Ana was pleased and I could see it.

'This is the future,' said Pedro portentously. 'We must celebrate, but first let's eat and drink.'

'Wait, I must wash my hands with running water in the sink.'

I turned the tap on lovingly, and roiled and moiled my hands in the glorious jet of clear water. Rarely had I taken so much pleasure in that simple ritual. I stepped outside the dimly lit bathroom into the dazzling daylight, and there on the way down to lunch I enjoyed a vision of El Valero with shooting fountains and chuckling rills, silver-tapped sinks spurting sweet water, and gently bubbling bidets.

Still, I brooded a little over Ana's denigration of my new water system. She was right; you couldn't really call it running water if you had to drive down to the river to fetch it. Pedro's description of the 'lost water' spring seemed like it might hold the answer. I decided to consult Domingo.

69

As ever, Domingo was happy to lend a hand and, furthermore, he knew the best spring and the best way to go about the job. Within a couple of days we had a concrete tank built to catch the water from a spring we had selected over on the other side of the valley. From it we ran rolls of polyethylene hose I had bought in Granada, down through the thickets of brambles and cane-breaks, out across the river, and up the hill to our house. There, with the aid of a stone and a piece of string, we connected the hose to the plastic water tank.

The next day the tank was ready to be filled and after a few hours of messing about with the air and *abejorros*, we had water gushing continuously from the taps. It seems fickle but from that moment my enchantment with the oil drum by the pomegranate tree, and its trickle of filthy water, evaporated.

Before long, we began to harbour thoughts of even greater indulgence – a hot shower in our own bathroom. Hitherto we had walked all the way across the valley to make use of Bernardo's. 'Feel free to come and use our shower whenever you want,' he had offered. 'There's a dead goat in it at the moment. Just try not to get soap on the goat, will you?'

There was indeed a goat hanging from the shower-pipe, spread-eagled without its skin and innards. The shower was the only place he could be sure that the flies wouldn't get at the meat, so there it hung until it was ready for the pot. It swung about jauntily and nudged you when you were least expecting it. Now prim and proper I am not, and it was very kind of Bernardo to let us share his bathroom facilities, but the goat pushed me fast in the direction of a water-heater of our own. The solution was simple. We went to Órgiva and bought one.

There was no stopping us now. We had running water, a heater, a cooker and a road. We were fast becoming slaves again to all the things we had come to this benighted spot to flee.

70

LOST ILLUSIONS

ANA AND I WANDERED ENDLESSLY AROUND THE FARM, EATING oranges and discussing what we might do with the various terraces and fields, what to change and what to leave, what to plant and what to grub up. Our relationship was already exhibiting signs of the primeval conflict between pastoralists and agriculturalists. Ana had visions of ordered rows of vegetables and fruit, neatly criss-crossed by well-tended walkways, a wilderness garden deep in wild flowers, with daffodils and cyclamen nodding on the grassy banks of the *acequia*. My heart was set on the idea of a flock of sheep scuffling across our shared idyll, with me the shepherd striding after them in a cloud of dust. I discussed the sheep idea with Domingo. The conversation left him looking thoughtful.

There was little we could do, however, in those winter months but look on while Pedro conducted the day-to-day running of our farm. Admittedly this didn't amount to much more than feeding his pigs and then wandering around in the riverbed with

71

the cows and goats. Yet he managed to inject such an air of industrious self-importance into these tasks that I felt inhibited and left out. I liked Pedro. I liked hearing his fund of odd stories and incomprehensible jokes, and the knowledge he passed on about the farm, but slowly and inexorably I began to move towards Ana's point of view on how good it would be to have the place to ourselves.

Ana, for her part, had developed the habit of melting into whatever task she was undertaking, almost like a mirage, whenever Pedro happened to approach. This could have been dismissed as characteristic reserve on her part except that she was always open and attentive with the Melero family; taking time to stroll with Expira on her daily water-carrying trips to the spring, or listening with genuine interest to any gardening advice from Old Man Domingo. With Domingo, too, she discovered a natural sympathy. He seemed to forget his painful shyness in her company and they would talk animatedly together of plants, animals and country topics.

Pedro noted the distinction and it did little to improve the atmosphere of our immediate domestic circle. The evening meal, in particular, had become strained. Not that there was any spoken antagonism – everyone was scrupulously polite, passing round the *costa* bottle and offering first pickings at the oily potatoes – but it was beyond my social talents to prevent a cloying silence descending. Beaune did well out of these meals. Throwing scraps became our only light relief.

In the end it was Pedro's refusal to try anything other than *papas a lo pobre*, and our hankering after more varied fare, that gave us the excuse to edge apart. Two camps established themselves. Pedro prepared his potatoes over his twig fire, while we concocted more cosmopolitan dishes on the new gas cooker. I still walked down to share a glass or two of *costa* with him at the end of the meal but never managed to rekindle the easy cama-

72

raderie of the summer. Pedro invariably would break off in the middle of some discussion about the farm and lumber off to the store-room where he now slept entombed among his hams and sausages and dried peppers.

While he took pains to avoid any actual talk of leaving, Pedro would haul out bits of his paraphernalia to load onto the Landrover whenever it looked as if we might be driving into town. Odd pieces of wood, bent rusty poles, tangled gobbets of wire and numberless artefacts made of esparto grass, rope, sacking, leather and string were carefully packed and placed in the back for us to offload with Maria at the other end. And with each journey Pedro's presence diminished a tiny bit.

One day he piled his horse with flowers and pots – the place was festooned with gay geraniums, cacti and succulents, sprouting exuberantly from rusty paint-cans, oil-drums and breeze-blocks – and stuffed the panniers so full that I thought the poor horse would collapse. Then, clutching a favourite cactus in a terracotta pot, he heaved his own great bulk onto the top of the load, cracked his stick across the animal's fleshless flanks, and lurched down the valley towards the town.

We didn't see Pedro again for almost a week, and as the days passed I became aware of how daunted he made me feel. For the first time since we had arrived, we felt the farm was truly our own and the realisation left each of us almost light-headed.

Ana was the first to seize the initiative. She suggested we sow some vegetables. We ran a hose from the tank down to the terrace below the track and there decided to create our plot. Pedro's system was an odd one; there seemed, so far as I could gather, to be different vegetables scattered about in different fields and terraces all over the farm. In his years at El Valero he had established which particular patch suited each vegetable best. So there was a patch of onions growing on the terrace by the Cádiar river; the peppers, hot ones, mild ones, bell ones, little leathery ones, grew in a triangle in the field above; potatoes grew down in the fields that bordered the other river and the garlic occupied an idyllic spot by the waterfall.

It gave the place an Eden-like quality, in that as you wandered among fruit trees, knee-deep in grass and flowers, you would come across a potato or perhaps an aubergine; these latter grew in a sunny spot beside the apricot tree. The disadvantage of the system was that it was impossible to work on the vegetables in any concerted fashion and it was a constant battle to keep the foraging beasts out of the crops. Pedro had weighed up the pros and cons and decided in favour of the Eden option. We decided to clump everything together on one terrace and see how it went.

The soil was stony and dry, and it needed a lot of hard chopping with the mattock to break down. It was heavy work but we attacked it with ferocious enthusiasm, and little by little transformed a part of the unpromising patch to a fine workable tilth in which to sow our beans. We both felt deeply satisfied with this first attempt to start running the farm along our own lines.

With a long groan I straightened up to stretch my back and looked straight into the eyes of Pedro, who was standing, mouth open, on the track above us. Ana, kneeling beside me, bent her head lower to the task.

'The Host! You can't grow vegetables there.'

'Why not?'

'The soil's wrong – too much *launa* on that terrace . . . and not enough sun. Look, it's all shaded by those oranges and olives.'

'Yes, but it's half past five in the evening . . .'

'And what's that you're sowing?'

'Beans.'

'What beans?'

'Broad beans.'

'They'll be no good.'

'Why not, for heaven's sake?'

'Wrong phase of the moon.'

Not a flicker from Ana as she trowelled in yet another bean.

'Look at this, too – you don't make ridges like that. Here, I'll show you how.' And down he came with his mattock, grunting with each blow as along went the ridge as if by magic.

'You must sow your peppers this week,' he said and disappeared up the track to the house.

All rural occupations in the Alpujarras have their allotted day, with the odd adjustment to accommodate the waxing and waning of the moon or the falling of a Friday. Thus the year always starts with the sowing of garlic on the 1st of January; then you prune your vines on the 24th or 25th depending on where you live. Most tasks are governed by the saint's day, as are many meteorological and cosmic phenomena such as the disappearance on St John's Day of the clouds of horseflies that plague the village of Fregenite.

The system is perfectly logical. It's a lot easier to remember a saint's day, which is something that everybody has had drummed into them from birth, than a mere date. Thus the enormous burden of information which unlettered peasants must keep in their heads is reduced. With the assistance of the saints they know by heart what should be done and when.

For one reason or another – bad organisation, forgetfulness, laziness – I don't always get the day quite right. Last year I was

75

pruning vines on January 29, rather pleased with myself for being so close to the right day. Josefina from the village was passing by. She stopped and watched me censoriously for a minute.

'You should prune vines on the 25th.'

'I know, but I'm only four days late. That's not too bad, is it?'

'We always prune ours on the 25th, rain or shine; that way we don't get any pests or diseases.'

'You mean you don't have to use any sprays and chemicals?'

'Are you mad? We blast them with every fungicide and pesticide we can lay our hands on.'

By which you can see how important it is to get the day right.

One morning, after a long time ratching around in the various sheds, stables and stores with which El Valero is honeycombed, Pedro turned up on our terrace where we were breakfasting on muesli, a thing he couldn't abide. He had come to take his leave. Shuffling and looking bashfully down, he held out a couple of bits of wood adzed to a vague shape and notched at each end.

'These are for you. You may have them as a parting gift.'

'Well thank you very much, Pedro . . . what are they?'

'Why, they're *camalas*, of course. I made them myself.'

'And what do you do with them?'

76 'You hang your pigs on them.'

'Ah – thank you.'

'This too,' he mumbled. 'This is for you. I've wrapped it in a plastic bag for reasons of hygiene.'

I reached carefully for the gift he held in his outstretched hand. It was quite obviously a brick. 'And what's this?' I asked, modulating my voice in keeping with the solemnity of the occasion.

'It's a brick,' he said, as if he'd just given me the keys to his women's quarters. 'You put it there and it stops that window banging in the wind.'

'Many, many thanks, Pedro, for these gifts. I shall always think of you when I use this brick and these . . . er . . . *camelas*?'

'*Camalas* . . . '

Then he turned to walk away.

'Wait, Pedro,' I cried, surprised to be confronted by his back while still fumbling for words of farewell. 'You can't just go like this.'

Pedro paused and studied me expectantly. So did Ana. I plunged on regardless. 'You know you're always welcome here with us. Why, you must treat this as your own home from home.'

Pedro grunted.

'El Valero won't feel the same without you. Isn't that true, Ana?'

'It won't indeed,' she answered a little ambiguously.

'Bah! It's time I was gone,' he growled. 'What use have you for an old man like me about the farm? I'd only get in the way of all these new plans of yours.'

He untied his horse and I followed him down the track, racking my brains for some way to inject some warmth into this leave taking.

'Here, hold this while I get up.' He handed me the headrope.

'But surely you'll come and see us?' I asked.

'Maybe, maybe not. I'll send Pepe up for the pigs. Give them a bucket of figs each, will you? And don't forget the water.' Then he set off down the hill. I think he added 'Walk with God,' but I couldn't be sure.

And that was it – no last piece of advice, no invitation to visit him in town, not even a farewell wave. I stood watching his large frame swing down towards the river, numbed by the abruptness of his departure. All manner of sentimental speeches surged uselessly to mind.

77

Ana broke my reverie by placing a consoling arm around my shoulder. 'It's time he went,' she said quietly, 'and it's far better that he choose the moment than wait for us to ask him to leave.'

'I know, Ana,' I answered, 'but I never expected him to go like this. He's acting as if we've become strangers to each other.'

'He's piqued, that's all. You couldn't expect Pedro to give up his hold on the farm in good grace, could you? He did at least make some sort of effort.'

That Ana found his behaviour explicable while I was awash with confusion was hardly a comfort.

'I'll take him a flagon of really good *costa* on my next trip to Órgiva, he'll like that,' I promised myself and, cheered a little by this resolution, hefted my new mattock onto my shoulder and went off to clear some brambles. As he did with just about every-thing else I bought, Pedro had told me that my mattock *no sirve* – it'd be no good. Wrong-shaped head.

∾

As it turned out I never did take Pedro that flagon of fine *costa*, nor have I ever visited him in town. Within days of his leaving the valley, I heard more than enough to destroy all my fond illu-sions about our friendship. Pepe delivered the first blow. He came with his tractor to fetch the pigs. Having helped him lash them to the trailer I invited him in for a beer and enquired eagerly how Pedro was settling into his home.

'Look,' he said. 'I know Romero a lot better than you do, and I'm telling you that you've wasted more than enough time with the man. He's just been taking advantage of you, I know because he's been boasting about it in town.'

I couldn't leave it there, I had to press him for details.

'Well, he's been saying that he's had this stupid foreigner eating

78

out of his hand and that he's been helping himself to whatever he wanted from the farm for months because you were too soft to stop him.' I stared at Pepe in amazement. He continued, but his next words were addressed largely to the dregs of his beer glass. 'And he's been saying things about Ana, too – crazy things. He's got this notion that she fancies him and that you're jealous about it . . . no, it's serious,' he added earnestly as I spluttered into my beer. 'Of course, no one believes a word, but I really wouldn't trust him up here again. It's not fair to Ana. You should tell him to keep right away from the Cortijo.'

With that awful clarity that comes when your self-delusions have just collapsed in a heap, I knew that Pepe was right. Now that Pedro had given up the farm, he was quite capable of dismissing us with the utmost contempt. I knew this because I had heard him speak in the same way about countless others. Odd that it had never struck me as heartless before.

Pepe was studying me with concern. 'Ask Domingo,' he urged. 'He'll give you the same advice.' I didn't need to. For once I was considering Pedro from Ana's point of view, with all her doubts corroborated. 'Don't worry, Pepe,' I muttered. 'I've heard it all before. You're not the first person who has tried to warn me about Pedro.'

It was true. Besides Ana, almost everyone I knew – Isabel, Domingo, Encarna, Georgina – had hinted that I was being too trusting or indulgent towards Romero, although none of them had ever backed their case with much detail. You don't easily spread ill-feeling about a neighbour, no matter how much you might dislike him. Once he had left the farm, however, our neighbours lost their reluctance to tell us what they knew of him. Listening as one sorry tale followed another, I started to realise how alone I had been in my estimation of him.

Ana was the only one who showed me any sympathy. 'I think

you brought out the best in him, Chris,' she said. 'He really seemed to enjoy impressing you and he did it so well. No wonder you were taken in.'

'But Ana, how could I have been such a lousy judge of character?' I groaned.

'Because you don't much care to judge people's characters,' she answered after a moment's thought. 'It's a strength, you know, as well as a weakness.'

It was small consolation.

DOMINGO AND THE SEARCH FOR BEAMS

IT WAS NOT LONG AFTER THE PIGS HAD FOLLOWED PEDRO TO town that Domingo paid his first visit to the house. We had always assumed that he had avoided crossing our threshold out of shyness or some obscure article of etiquette. It hadn't occurred to us that the Melero family objected to visiting Pedro and had been waiting for him to leave before indulging their curiosity as to what we were up to.

Proudly, I showed Domingo our innovations with the running water and the heater in the bathroom. He nodded, showing that he had no absolute objection to the apparatus. But the wooden bed – that was a mistake. We'd be eaten alive in a bed like that.

Domingo then took out his knife and jabbed it into a ceiling beam. 'It's rotten,' he declared, illustrating the point by dislodging a shower of dust and mouldy splinters. 'The *launa* hasn't been raked and the water's seeped through. It could fall about your ears at any moment.'

'Oh Lord, do you think they're all like that?' I asked, wondering what had happened to neighbourly small-talk.

'No. Only a few beams are rotten right through but you might as well replace the lot. Chestnut's the thing for roofing beams. I know where we can find a good supply.'

And thus the job was conceived. Our first winter remains with me now as one long search for roofing beams. Domingo fell naturally into the role of guide, introducing me to my new world of villages and mountains as we ranged to and fro in search of this elusive but desirable building material.

~

Alpujarran architecture is a simple affair consisting of the more or less orderly re-arrangement of the materials that either grow to hand or lie randomly scattered around. The proportions are dictated by a simple equation; the width is the maximum supporting capacity of a chestnut, poplar or eucalyptus beam, with a thick layer of wet *launa* (the oily grey almost waterproof clay that runs in seams throughout the Alpujarras) on top. This comes to approximately three and a half metres. The height is limited by the extent to which an Alpujarran man can lift stones, and, as most are short of stature, rarely exceeds one metre eighty from floor to beam-seats. Length is curtailed by the groundspace available and windows are calculated to let in just enough light to grope around in at midday, while excluding the extraneous rays that might otherwise consume the inhabitants. The whole, in a village, has to mesh with a mass of other similar dwellings huddled like the hexagons of a beehive. What you end up with is something between a square box and a stone railway carriage.

When my mother first saw a photograph of my newly purchased home she was appalled. 'I had hoped that you might end up living in a Queen Anne house,' she lamented. 'I've always liked Queen Anne. But here you are, living in . . . living in what I can only describe as a stable.'

To be honest, elegance and sophistication are not the adjectives that spring to mind when describing Alpujarran architecture. The charm of the style lies in its simplicity. The variations on the basic design and the simple ornament that the inhabitants add to their homes often result in creations of great beauty. The first time I saw Alpujarran architecture I was unimpressed but slowly it wheedled its way into my heart, and now . . . well, I should feel very uncomfortable indeed living behind leaded windows beneath a gabled roof.

The simple box-type structure is identical to that found in the Berber villages of Morocco – it was the Berbers who brought this kind of building to the region – and similar to all the vernacular architecture of the Middle East. Its great advantage is its cheapness. The doors and windows are the only parts of a house that have to be bought for money; the rest has merely to be hewn or hacked down, or gathered and hauled up from the river.

The walls are stone, mortared with mud, and should have a minimum thickness of sixty centimetres, preferably a metre. This keeps out heat in the summer and cold in the winter. The lintels and beams are wooden, eucalyptus or poplar if you live down in the river valleys, or sweet chestnut, the best of all, if you live above a thousand metres where the chestnut forests girdle the high villages. In the Low Alpujarra a mat of canes is fixed on top of the beams. The canes are lashed together with woven ropes of esparto grass which grows wild everywhere. The canes too grow in abundance in the rivers, as do the trees for the beams. On the cane mat is laid a thick layer of brush – oleander, genista, broom, thyme – and then finally comes the layer of *launa*. You should always lay your *launa* during the waning moon to get it to settle properly and give you as watertight a roof as possible – but, of course, never on a Friday.

83

A hundred years ago the stone walls would have been left bare, but these days most of the houses are whitewashed, outside and in. There are two reasons for this: it reduces the heat inside by several degrees on a hot summer day; and the lime, particularly the *cal viva* that comes in the form of white rocks that you must steep in a drum of water, where they hiss and bubble, has a strong disinfectant effect.

~

It was a bitterly cold day when we set off in search of beams. We headed west towards Lanjarón and then wound up a steep track by the river. I eased the old Landrover gently around bend after bend, higher and higher, until we ran out of road altogether. Domingo, with a thin jacket thrown over his shirt as a sole concession to the weather, leapt out to greet an elderly shepherd who had stepped from beneath the trees to watch us pass. We were in luck, it seemed; the old man had just that moment been thinking of selling off a load of chestnut for beams. He jabbed a gnarled index finger towards a patch of forest on a ridge near the skyline.

Onwards and upwards we clambered beneath the dappled shade of huge trees. There were patches of snow among the fallen leaves and ice on the banks of the river. Our friend's chestnut forest was in a magnificent spot, not far beneath the high snow-peaks and with a view of the sea way to the south, but the wood was no good. A fire had recently rampaged through that section of the mountain, leaving the trees half-deadened and black, and their girth was mostly enormous. We were looking for a hundred beams. Domingo reckoned there was not a dozen to be had in all that expanse of forest. Chestnuts must be coppiced and looked after to make good building material. This wood had

84

been utterly neglected. And besides there was the cutting and carting to think of. It was a long and difficult journey for a mule to carry each beam down to the nearest point of access for a lorry. We thanked the owner for his time and returned to the valley.

'If you want beams,' said a man in a bar, 'then Martín of Trevélez is your man. He has hundreds.'

So we drove to Trevélez to track down Martín, whose beams turned out to be ready cut and stacked by the river. The price he was asking sounded reasonable enough and, leaving us to inspect his stack, he said that if we wanted to discuss terms he would be in the bar in the square at two. We did not join him. Every one of the beams was rotten: chewed over by worms, ravished by mephitic fungi, or twisted or knotty or thick. 'He'll have a job to sell that lot for firewood,' Domingo commented.

Still, it had been an enjoyable trip, and we had some ham and some wine in Trevélez before setting out on the high mountain road home. It was then that Domingo, as ever, surprised me. 'My uncle Eduardo has chestnut woods above Capileira,' he said. 'He'd be keen to sell you some beams.'

'Why didn't you say anything about him before?' I asked.

'Oh, it's interesting to see what other beams there are about and I always enjoy a trip to Trevélez. Besides, Eduardo wouldn't have been home until now. We can go and visit him now, on the way back.'

And so we did, turning off and up towards Capileira, highest of the three villages of the Poqueira Gorge. It's a pretty place, with little white box-like houses huddled around a church like chicks beneath a hen's wing. But it's the setting that steals your breath. From high on the terraced slopes of the gorge the horizon spreads north over the great white cirque of Veleta, a soft stole of cloud nestling below its peaks. To the south, a wide mountain pass opens onto the Mediterranean and on a clear winter's day you can just about make out the peaks of the Rif Mountains across the straits in Morocco.

For some years now the village has been a popular retreat for artists and bohemians from as far afield as Japan and Mexico, although it is still mostly inhabited by the indigenous agricultural population. This ensures that the lanes are kept spattered with a fragrant coating of mule and sheep turds, and that tucked among the gorgeous renovated dwellings you still find the cruder contrivances of the indigenous inhabitants for housing chickens and pigs.

The strains of Debussy were floating from a newly carpentered window as we made our way across the main square and along a narrow, cobbled alley. Domingo knocked on the heavy studded wooden door of a shabby but pretty village house. It was opened by a dark bundle of a woman who exclaimed in delight at her unexpected visitor.

'Come in, nephew, come in,' she cried, pulling Domingo forward, with both hands clamped around his shoulders. 'It's not often we see you up here. Let me look at you. Ah, so handsome and yet what good is a face like this if you refuse to find yourself a wife?' She emphasised the point by grabbing fiercely at his cheek.

Domingo smiled and bent to kiss her, apparently used to this sort of welcome. Behind her, in a dimly lit room, three or four men were leaning over a steaming pot stabbing at bits of goat meat with their knives.

'I've brought you this foreigner, my new neighbour Cristóbal,' Domingo announced.

The knives hung momentarily in the air as the group of men turned to stare at me.

'An honour, much pleasure, enchanted,' growled the eldest of them, whom I took to be Eduardo. From what I could make out

86

in the gloom, there was a strong family resemblance between this man and at least two of the other men grouped around the table. They were lean as nails, short, sinewy and clearly used to hard work and weather. Each had a nose so prominent that their other facial features seemed to skulk in its shadow.

'Come and eat goat,' commanded Eduardo, clattering back his chair to make room for us at the table. Domingo took out his pocket-knife, a long blade with an edge like a razor, and began slicing and stabbing at the meat as others were doing. Uncertainly, I drew my own knife from my pocket – a pruning knife, rounded at the end and blunt – and tried in vain to skewer a few bony lumps. I didn't tell them that from my earliest years my mother had forbidden me utterly to eat from my knife and that I hadn't developed the skill.

The company stopped eating and watched me with interest. 'You do it like this, Cristóbal,' offered Domingo, but Eduardo had lost patience with his inept guest. 'Give the man a fork and bring him some wine, woman,' he ordered, 'He can't eat, he's dry.'

A glass of *costa* appeared. Eduardo looked at me steadily as I took a swig. 'My nephew tells me that you've got a machine for shearing sheep,' he ventured. 'People round here say such things fry your flock.'

An animated discussion began. I spoke a little boastfully of shearing hundreds of sheep in a day with the foreign gadget. Domingo said he'd give it a try come the spring. The others seemed less convinced. Then Domingo, as if to clinch the matter, threw in the information that I played the guitar.

This brought an enthusiastic thump on the table from Eduardo. 'Hah! Now you're talking. Manuel, we have a musician in the house. Bring out the guitars.'

Manuel did as he was told, handing one to his father and then sitting beside him with the other. They tuned up roughly, fingered some chords and lolloped into an Alpujarran folk tune.

87

Now, much as I would like to write of how Orpheus himself never plucked a string as exquisitely as those work-hardened fingers of old Eduardo, and of how I was spellbound by the earthy players' mastery of their instruments and by the simple loveliness of the song, I cannot deny the truth. The music was a foul dirge and its progress marred by venomous oaths from Eduardo as Manuel unerringly missed his cue. Father and son scowled at each other throughout the performance, consumed with spleen at the other's incompetence.

At last the dreadful thing came to a close. 'Beautiful,' I sighed. 'You don't know any more, do you?'

Eduardo and Manuel examined me through narrowed eyes.

'Alright, give him another . . .'

It served me right. I speared a piece of goat and pretended to be carried away by the beat, tapping my foot in a futile attempt to pick out a rhythm. As I tapped I masticated furiously at the detestable lump of goat-gristle in my mouth. The song shuddered to its demise and the players once again eyed me inquisitively. But this time my integrity as a music critic was saved by the goat-gristle which had conveniently lodged itself in my windpipe. One half of the rubbery lump was stuck halfway down while the other, joined to the first by a strong piece of animal elastic, remained in my mouth. I burbled and spluttered while everyone looked on in consternation.

88

'Drink wine. Hit him on the back. No, give him water. Give him bread . . .'

Something must have worked because I managed at last to reunite the two ends and gain breath, though not enough to deliver my opinion of their latest piece.

'Now you do it,' said Eduardo, handing me the guitar with a hint of menace in his voice.

'Oh, I'm really not fit to . . . It would be difficult to follow that last piece . . . I only really play for myself.'

'Play, man – play!'

I played.

'He can play,' they nodded to one another.

I played some very basic flamenco, very badly.

'He plays Spanish music.'

As I struggled to the end of my piece, wincing at the wrong notes and bodged fingerings, I realised that nobody was listening anyway. Domingo was telling them of my plans to run a flock of sheep at El Valero.

'Sheep? Down there? They'll roast. You can't keep sheep in the valleys. Goats yes, but sheep – sheep are not meant to be kept in hot river valleys. If you want sheep you should give them to us to look after for you. They'll be happy here in the cool of the mountains. We can make a good price for you. We've got endless grazing up here.'

Domingo looked at me meaningfully. 'Sheep do fine in the valleys,' he said.

'What do you know about sheep, cousin? You haven't enough sheep to graze in a flower pot!'

'There are plenty of good-sized flocks around Órgiva,' Domingo answered. 'They never come up to the tops and they do perfectly alright.'

'All that heat and dust – it's a shame for a sheep. There's no air to breathe.'

This was standard talk from mountain shepherds but, as Domingo had said, there were indeed large flocks down in the valleys. They never went to the mountains in the summer and still they thrived.

We moved on to the subject of chestnut beams.

'Why, we have a whole forest full, just above the old abandoned village. You'll need to cut them but they're good beams, and there's a good mule-track to the village from there. Four hundred pesetas a metre is all I'm asking.'

89

It seemed a very fair deal so the next day we went to inspect the beams. They were just what we needed and as December drew to a close, Domingo and I made frequent journeys to the forest, to scramble about in the crisp, clear mountain air with the chain-saw. We would make a day of these expeditions, admiring the view while cooking sausages and *tocino* over a wood fire.

THE TIME OF *MATANZAS*

WINTER IN THE ALPUJARRAS IS THE SEASON FOR *MATANZAS* OR pig killings. Any other time and the flies and wasps would amass in a frenzy of looting and spoil the neighbourly business of slaughter. For the same reason the day's grim deed starts early in the cool of the morning.

There were four *matanzas* in the valley during our first winter, beginning with Manolo's down at El Granadino near the entrance to the gorge. His pigs were to be dispatched between Christmas and New Year. I remembered Manolo well from my ride as bonded foreigner on Pedro's old nag. Unlike most of the new acquaintances I had made that day, he had insisted on being introduced to me by name and even lingered on to exchange a few words in carefully enunciated Spanish. Such kindness left a deep impression. So when Domingo brought word that we would be welcome to attend Manolo's *matanza*, I was more than inclined to go along.

Ana was less sure. She could think of few good reasons to prise herself out of bed before dawn on a nippy winter's morning, and witnessing the death throes of a pig was certainly not one of them. However, duty to one's neighbour is an argument that rarely fails with Ana (suspending for a moment the possibility that one's neighbour's pigs might also have a claim) and on the appointed day we stirred early from the matrimonial bed and headed down the river.

Seven on a winter's morning in the riverbed is cold. With nowhere else to go, all the cold air in the mountains gathers at the bottom of the valley and contrives to numb and freeze the extremities of any traveller who might happen along. For a brief moment, though, it is also very beautiful. As the first rays of the morning sun touch the high cliffs of the Contraviesa, they shine rose and gold and the gentle light floods the curves and folds of the hills below. It somehow frees your mind from the preoccupations it might have with the early symptoms of frostbite.

The sun was still way below the cliffs of the gorge when we arrived at El Granadino, but fires had already been lit and blue curls of woodsmoke rose into the cold air. The quiet of the morning was broken by the sound of men droning on about vegetables and hunting escapades, and women belabouring chickens and children.

We climbed onto the patio where everybody stood up to shake our hands very formally before Manolo, with the same studied attention to syllables, ushered us towards two straight-backed chairs in a dark room. A twig fire smoked quietly in the corner. The men were fortifying themselves with anis, brandy and sweet cakes – difficult stuff to get down so early in the morning, but it seemed that to kill a pig you needed a deep lode of alcohol coursing around the system.

Ana, being a foreigner, was exonerated from the drudgesome lot of the women – the washing-up, the serving and preparation

92

of dainties – and admitted into the august company of the men and their conversation about the pigs and other animals they had killed. She didn't contribute much to the talk as she had never killed a pig, and her thoughts about hunting would hardly have been welcome. So she stifled a couple of yawns while I nursed my second anis and grappled with that vertiginous feeling you get when you'd like to join in but know that you have nothing to say.

Soon the men tired of the cakes and liquor.

'*A la faena!* On with the job!'

We all trooped out in manly fashion to kill four enormous pigs.

Now to persuade a pig to come out of its sty and be killed is a desperate business. The owner goes inside and with sweet words attempts to cajole the pig into allowing him to slip a noose round its trotter. He then tries to pull the pig from the cosy darkness of its pit out into the glaring sunlight of a yard filled with men hooting encouragement, where great pots of water are bubbling, hot fires are smoking and gleaming knives clash against the sharpening-stones. Of course he can never achieve this, as the pig is not only understandably reluctant to go but also weighs a good hundred kilos, most of it solid muscle. It digs its three free trotters into the mud and refuses to budge.

Everybody knows this is going to happen because it always does happen. Yet everybody always knows better than everybody else what should have been done to prevent it. Eventually, with four men on the rope, and two behind controlling the tail, the poor creature is hauled into the open.

The pig-killing table is ready. The pig-killer stands by with his terrible hook. An upward thrust and the hook jabs in, deep into the underjaw. The pig shrieks and becomes powerless. It can only follow the merciless hook. The killer drags the pig alongside the table and the men all gather round. They grab it by the arms

93

and legs and tail and heave it up onto the rough boards, kicking and squealing. Ropes lash it into position where it subsides into a sort of despairing resignation.

'Bring the buckets; wash the neck; here with the hose!'

There's a lull as the pig heaves quietly and the killer pokes about under its throat to find the propitious spot for the knife-thrust. Blish! In goes the knife – a twist – and the blood gushes into the bucket, stirred by a stout woman to stop it clotting. The pig heaves and lashes out and whinnies, and the men who are leaning on the pig to persuade it to stay on the table look at one another with knowing looks as it goes limp and the life passes from the body. Then one of them gives it a slap to signal that the worst is over.

'That's good and gone, then.'

Everybody relaxes their grip.

It's a horrible business, and the very thought of that hook makes me shiver, but there's an undeniable fascination to the slaughter as well: that same mix of repulsion and excitement that you find at bullfights. And there comes a moment when the horror of the thing evaporates. All of a sudden the living creature shrieking out its last breaths becomes an inanimate leather bag, a thing you can poke at with almost no compunction.

A strange bonhomie emerges at this time. Faces taut with tension relax into broad smiles and a ribald humour bubbles out. Even the most shy or taciturn in the group bandy jokes or allow themselves the odd snigger as they lay into the leather bag, scorching it with brands of bolina, an oily bush that burns like a blowtorch, and scraping off the burnt hairs. After twenty minutes of tolerable hard work with the knives flashing and the bolina blazing, in goes the *camala* and the dead pig is hoisted aloft just above dog-height for the killer to gut and split.

Then the women appear with their bowls to catch each organ or piece of tripe that comes slithering out and whisk it away to

94

start the long process of transforming it into a panoply of sausages – *longaniza, salchichón, chorizo, chicharrones, tocino, morcilla,* and so on.

By this stage it is reckoned that the men are in need of sustenance so a feast of *chicharrones* is brought out, and washed down with anis and *costa. Chicharrones* are the fatty excrescences which appear all the way along the long intestine. Fried in olive oil until the outside is crispy, they are absolutely delicious, and they are better still on their reappearance as a cake – *torta de chicharrones* – a big, sweet, sumptuous doughy bun, shot through with gobbets of intestine fat. I looked around for Ana to share this gastronomic delight but she had her back to me, rather determinedly I thought, leaning over a bowl of offal that Expira was preparing.

And so we moved on to the next pig, which happened more or less as the first had – a little more efficiently in that the team were getting their eye in, though the advantage was lessened by a steady course towards alcoholic oblivion. The sun dragged up over the hill, bathing the whole ghastly proceeding in warm light. The second pig dispatched, a third and then a fourth were pulled from the stable, hooked, jabbed, bled, scorched, scraped, split and hung. Round and round went the goatskin wine-bottle, washing down pig-fatty dishes. More improbable and fantastical became the tales of pig killings and feats of manly prowess.

Ana tapped my shoulder and gave me one of her old-fashioned looks as if to ask when this long ordeal would be over. I raised a heavy-lidded eye and tried to clear my brain of some heroic fantasy that had lodged itself where rational thought used to loiter. She seemed to be signalling to me from an immeasurable distance and the gestures were hard to decipher. My stomach felt as if a great glutinous stone had somehow found its way in and my head was thrumming, verging on a storm of a headache.

95

Just before darkness fell there was a general dispensation for everyone to go home to feed their pigs, shut their mules and chickens in, change clothes and come back for the real feasting. A pig or two is supposed to supply just about all the pigmeat needs of a family through the coming year, but it seemed to me that the whole lot was going to be wolfed by the guests and helpers on the first day. Still, I suppose there must be something left over.

Ana and I staggered back up the river in the fading light.

'You're not serious about going back, are you?'

'Well, I really think we ought to . . .'

'What, come all the way back down the river in the dark just to hear more of those ridiculous stories and eat that dreadful fatty muck? You must be bonkers!'

Ana is nothing if not honest. Sometimes also she is right.

'I must admit that at the moment I would rather die than let any member of the pig family or parts of it pass my lips. And I don't want any more wine either . . .'

'You certainly don't.'

'We might feel better about it in a couple of hours, let's see.'

In a couple of hours we were both fast asleep, dreaming of nut cutlets and spinach quiche, boiled cucumber and radishes with brown rice . . .

COUNTING SHEEP

IN SPRING THE BLOSSOMING OF THE ORANGE TREES TAKES YOU
unawares. At first only a pale haze becomes apparent across the
dark green of the leaves. This is the green of the flower-buds.
Then all of a sudden the buds are transformed into exquisite
white five-petalled stars, radiating from cream-yellow pistils and
stamens. The scent is delicate and heady, and when each tree
becomes a mass of white flowers an almost tangible mist of
orange blossom hangs in the air.

The blossom lasts for weeks, scenting April, May and June, and
all this time the trees are alive with the insistent buzzing of bees.
Then as the flowers wither a tiny green orange appears in the
centre of each one, a perfect miniature replica of the fully
formed fruit. Were each orangelet to grow its course, the average
tree would be laden with from twenty to thirty tons of fruit, but
the breezes, birds and the marvellous mechanisms of the tree
itself do their bit to cull them. The ground beneath becomes a

97

mosaic of flowers and orangelets. Our neighbours spread sheets beneath the trees to catch the flowers for orange blossom tea, *flor de azahara*, which apparently helps you to sleep.

The trees were reaching an early floral crescendo when Domingo swung his donkey, Bottom, up the hill towards the house. (Bottom is not, of course, the name Domingo uses for his beast. He calls it *burra* – donkey. But we dubbed it Bottom, one morning, and the literary and scatological associations have kept the name going for us.)

Our neighbour had some news to impart.

'My uncle Arsenio wants you to shear his sheep with that machine you keep in the stable. I told him he ought to. I said this is the way things are going to be in the future, so he might as well start now.'

This came as a surprise. 'But I thought your family were against the idea?' I reminded him.

'That was Eduardo, he knows nothing. No, Arsenio's willing to give it a go. His flock will be ready for us a week after tomorrow. He lives at Los Caracoles over there.' Domingo pointed above the trees towards the high hills.

This may not seem the most momentous of exchanges but it meant a great deal to me. I was, for the first time, being offered a part to play in the life of the Alpujarras. No longer would I be an outsider observing, but I could step inside the scene and become one of the observed. This was something I had yearned to do in all my years of travelling. Perhaps, if this really took off, I might even acquire an *apodo*, or nickname, like the locals: Cristóbal El Pelador – the peeler – had a nice ring to it. The money would be a help, too, if I got to do a number of flocks, and there was also the excitement of introducing something new. Few of the shepherds in the high valleys had witnessed the wonders of mechanised shearing and they would be looking to me to point out the path of progress.

I spent a happy week checking over my aged machinery and lapsing into vainglorious reveries whenever the bongling of a passing flock caught my ears.

~

The great day arrived and in the hazy light of an early May morning Domingo and I loaded the Landrover and set out for the High Alpujarra, stopping for a quick coffee in Órgiva to launch the journey.

At Soportújar we turned off the tarmac road and began a serpentine ascent along the *camino forestal,* a dirt track bordered by dusty cypresses and acacias, that leads into the hills. A dozen or more hairpin bends and we passed a painted wooden sign bearing the words O-Sel-Ling and a rough but well-trodden path winding up from the track. This was the turning to the Tibetan Buddhist monastery of Al Atalaya.

You may think that there's something askew with your organs of perception when, in a small Spanish agricultural town, one which sports beans and potatoes in the municipal flowerbeds, you come across a shaven-headed monk, trudging along in full burgundy robe and dusty boots. But in fact your eyes do not deceive you.

In 1985 a son was born in a Granada hospital to a Spanish Buddhist couple living in the Alpujarras. The boy, who was named Osel Hita Torres, 'Osel' meaning 'Clear Light' in Tibetan, was discovered to be the reincarnation of Lama Thubten Yeshe, one of Tibetan Buddhism's leading disseminators in the Western world, who had died eleven months earlier in California. Osel himself no longer graces his native soil, having been whisked off to Dharamsala, the seat of the Dalai Lama in exile. However, the monastery that was founded in his name thrives as a Buddhist retreat and temple of meditation, drawing countless Western

99

acolytes and the occasional exalted member of the Tibetan theocracy-in-waiting.

I peered about in the hopes of seeing one such holy man, but none materialised. Domingo, for whom Lama Buddhism was a subject of very little interest, hardly registered the monastery turning – though even he drew in his breath as we rounded the hill. Below us, flooded in morning light, spread the Poqueira gorge with its three lovely villages seeping blue woodsmoke into the still air.

We kept on climbing, past mountain meadows studded with poppies, margaritas, convolvulus and purple vetch, while the valleys and villages below grew blue and misty. I could see El Valero with its green river-fields far below us, perhaps four or five miles as the crow flies, but a good hour's drive. At last Domingo directed me to stop, beside a sheep yard on a steep hill. I turned the engine off and listened to the mountain sound-scape: distant goat bells and barking dogs, cocks crowing in the villages below, and larks and tutubias twittering high above the field where we stood.

Domingo was unusually quiet.

'I'm thinking,' he explained.

'What about?'

'My uncle Arsenio.'

'Oh?'

'He's a bad lot. We'll have to keep our eyes open. He'll find some way of cheating you for sure.'

'But he's your family.'

'He's still a bad lot. I don't know of anyone worse, really.'

'Thanks a lot, Domingo, seems like you've fixed me up with a real winner for a first job!'

'Don't worry, we'll keep an eye on him.'

∼

Arsenio was not in fact a blood relative of Domingo. He had been lucky enough to marry one of Expira's seven sisters who, for some reason best known only to themselves, deemed it desirable to gain influence in the high mountains by marrying shepherds. So Domingo is related through a network of influential aunts to everyone who is anyone in the Alpujarran sheep world. I couldn't have had a better introduction.

As Domingo expounded on his disreputable relations, we became aware of Arsenio's flock of sheep coming up for the shearing. They took shape as a pale blur against the dark of the trees, then came into focus as a sizable flock of sheep, with yapping dogs and shouting men at its edges. At that moment the last thing I felt like doing was to spend the day shearing sheep. I wanted to stroll through the meadows and head up towards the great fields of snow that skirted the peaks of the Sierra Nevada.

Also, to be honest, I was just a touch nervous about how the day was going to work out. 'You don't tie them up, then?' a shepherd had asked me earlier in the spring.

'Hell no! You can't shear a sheep when it's tied up.'

'But they'll jump and struggle and be up and bugger off.'

'Well, I must have shorn a hundred and fifty thousand sheep in my time and I've not had to tie one up yet.'

'Maybe so, but that's in foreign parts. Here the sheep are different; they're wild.'

Domingo had put the word about that this cocky foreigner was not only going to shear a hundred and fifty sheep in a day by himself . . . but he was going to do it without tying them up! Such hubris deserved a serious downfall.

'This your foreigner, then, Domingo? Does he speak Spanish?'

Arsenio was the very essence of Alpujarreño shepherd – tiny, sinewy and leathery brown. His knobbly features split into a grin as he pumped my arm vigorously.

'Lovely place you've got here, Arsenio.'

101

A look of utter bafflement came over his face.

'What's your foreigner say, Domingo?'

'He says he likes it here.'

'Heh heh, wonderful, marvellous. Right, let's eat something.'

'Er . . . we've just had breakfast actually. Couldn't we . . .'

'What's he saying, Domingo?'

It was pointless trying to communicate directly with Arsenio. He was of the persuasion – and he's not alone in this – that anyone who is not from the Alpujarras will be incomprehensible. He disconnected the moment I spoke, looking at Domingo as if I had said something disgusting, and waiting for him to repeat my words.

~

The news of my shearing machine had spread through high pastoral circles and quite a gathering had formed to watch the promised spectacle. Whoever heard of shearing a sheep without tying it up? Domingo had found himself a right madman for the job, that was for sure.

There were perhaps a dozen shepherds in attendance, all with sticks, all with hats and leather shoulder-bags, all with grubby fags of home-grown *churrasco* hanging on their lips, and all leering at me horribly.

102   I made a bit of a song and dance for the audience over setting up the gear: carefully positioning the board to shear on, inspecting the cables to the generator and heavy electric motor, and fiddling about in a box full of machinery parts. It's difficult to resist being a bit prima donna-ish at times.

'So that's it, is it? The shearing machine. How does it work, do you think?'

'It's done by the electric – and that's the harm of it. It shocks the sheep. Bloke over Dúrcal way had his sheep shorn by the electric and they all died, every one of them fried to a frazzle. You just wait.'

'Fernando of Torvizcón used a mechanical machine one year and it took so much wool off the sheep that they all got sunburn. It's not natural.'

'No, natural it ain't, and you've stuck your neck out here, Arsenio. I wonder how many sheep you'll have tomorrow,' added another shepherd with undisguised relish.

'It'll save a lot of work . . . ' I glanced from the corner of my eye to see who this modern-minded man was. '. . . and in a couple of years time there won't be a shepherd in the Alpujarra using hand-shears. You mark my words.'

The defector turned out to be José, Domingo's cousin, who often came to stay at the Melero household. He gave me a little courage. 'I don't think there's any danger of either electrocution or sunstroke,' I assured the crowd.

Twelve moist cigarette butts swivelled towards Domingo and quivered as they spoke: 'What's he saying, Domingo?'

I gave a hitch to my trousers, checked the machine, and dived for the first sheep, tipping her with a practised flip onto her bum, ready for the shears.

'You wait, she'll kick the eggs off the bugger, serve him right!'

But as luck would have it, the sheep turned nicely and sat meekly between my knees. I pulled the cord. The shears zinged into life and I plunged them into the wool. It peeled off like butter, the sheep perfectly compliant and co-operative. About forty-five seconds – there wasn't much wool on her – and I helped her to her feet with a neat pressure of the right knee. A professional-looking twist to the tension head on the shears . . .

'What seems to be the hold-up? Where's the next sheep?'

103

The first sheep of a day's shearing hurts. All your limbs are stiff and you can only reach the distant bits of rump and tail with the greatest effort. But it only takes one sheep to warm up. The second sheep of the day is a pleasure – all your energy and strength are there to help and just moving through the various postures of the first sheep has loosened up all the necessary muscles in your body.

The trouble, though, is that after the first three, or perhaps five, the repetitiveness of the job starts to get to you. There is a set technique. Each sheep is put through an identical series of positions and the cutter passes over the body in a more or less identical series of strokes, or 'blows' as they're known in the trade. It takes about fifty blows to shear a fully woolled sheep. These sparsely woolled mountain ones took about twenty. I could have done the job in my sleep.

By the time you get to the fiftieth sheep the boredom gets spiced by jabs of pain as the muscles in your lower back begin to burn and scream a bit. Top class shearers, the sort who shear four hundred sheep a day, seven days a week, suffer from woolburn. The friction of the wool passing over the back of the cutting hand takes all the skin off the knuckles and they bleed constantly. In Spain the main enemies are heat and dust. You can't work in the sun; it sucks the energy from you in a matter of minutes. But even in the shade you work drenched in sweat and eventually become tarred and feathered with dung-dust and wisps of wool.

104

~

Another sheep was brought to the board and away I went. Domingo crouched beside me, watching intently; the crowd muttered and mumbled amongst themselves. This sheep had a tail. Most sheep are docked, for reasons that I won't go into here.

Tails are awful. It can cost you a good ten seconds of excruciating bending to do a tail. What's difficult is getting the wool off the tip, because that's the part you hold it by and you have to steer clear of your fingers.

'Leave the tip of the tail on,' said Domingo. 'It's the custom here to leave a great clump of wool on the tip. Helps with the flies.'

So I did. It made the job much easier. I couldn't resist a smirk, though, at the sight of all those shorn sheep with their poodle-cut tails. Arsenio and Pepe, darting in and out of the flock to grab each new sheep for the shearing, had pained looks on their faces.

'What's the matter? Shearing not good enough for you?'

'What's he saying, Domingo?'

'I haven't a clue.'

The sun rose higher in the sky; the sweat ran off me and onto the sheep; the pile of grubby wool beside me grew higher, and the proportion of shorn poodle-tails to woolly ones steadily increased. I sheared what seemed like a hundred or so and then we stopped for lunch.

Pepe's wife Angustias, who was about three times as big as he was, had lumbered up from their farm way below, laden with bags and baskets of provisions. Ana had turned up, too, and was surveying the scene still flushed from her long climb. We washed our hands in a nearby stream and sat down to a picnic in the shade of a huge cherry tree.

105

Sheep-shearing is a grimy old job, but it does take you to some beautiful places. We gazed up towards the immense snow-covered crags of the cirque of Veleta under a sky the colour of cornflowers. Angustias passed round some bottles of what is euphemistically known as 'coarse country wine', and some beer that had been cooling in the stream, and laid out a spread of olives and omelette, sausages of various denominations, *jamón* and bread.

'You are the one doing the work, Cristóbal, you must eat more,' she urged, 'before this lazy lot finish it all.'

'No, I'd love to – thank you very much – it's quite delicious, but I find it hard to bend down and work if I've eaten too much.'

Angustias understood foreigners perfectly well.

'Perhaps you can explain something to me?' she began. 'I meet a lot of foreigners right here at the farm. They get off the bus in the village and then get lost looking for that monastery of theirs. They look so starved and yet when I give them some *tocino* like this,' and she pointed at some wodges of pig fat presented with all the delicacy of a plate of petit fours, 'or maybe a nice piece of *chorizo* they just push it to the side of the plate and nibble at the bread. Why do they do this, when they seem so hungry?'

'If they're looking for the monastery then they're probably Buddhists, and *tocino* may not have quite the same appeal for them as it does for you and me.'

'Buddhists you say . . . well, perhaps they are, but what in the name of the Virgin do they put in their stomachs? They all look so thin and pale, like they lived under stones. A gust of wind could blow them away.'

'So far as I know they eat boiled vegetables, and brown rice, and as a special treat perhaps some nuts.'

'Ay the poor things, what a terrible life. Though perhaps it would be better for me if I also ate a bit less. I'd like to be small and slim like you, Ana, but what can I do? I do so love the white meat of the ham. Do you think that it is so very fattening?'

'Perhaps it is a little,' said Ana, gazing with feminine fellow feeling at Angustias' massive body. 'Yes, the white meat of the ham is not the thing for slimming.'

I got up, stretched and looked without enthusiasm over the gate at the fifty-odd sheep that were left to shear. It was time to start work again so I flapped carefully down the hill in my shearing moccasins to turn the generator on. When I arrived,

Domingo was on the board with a sheep, holding it more or less right and shearing it more or less efficiently.

'You've done this before, Domingo.'

'No, but it can't be that difficult, and I've been watching you all morning.' In not more than a couple of minutes the sheep was done and happily scratching itself with the rest of the flock. Domingo grabbed another one and sheared it without too much difficulty, and pretty neatly too.

'Come on, man, I don't believe you've never done this before. It takes years to do it that well.'

'Well, I've done a few with the hand-shears, tying them up and that, but this is a much better way of doing it.'

That afternoon he sheared about a dozen sheep, without sweating and without his back hurting. For a beginner that really is pretty remarkable.

'I'll buy you a second-hand machine from England and we'll set up and shear the sheep of the Alpujarras together.'

'If you like.' Domingo is nothing if not phlegmatic.

By early evening we had finished and the flock rushed gladly from the stable to graze for a couple of hours in the meadows where the shadows of the trees were already growing longer.

'One hundred and forty-seven sheep. How much?' asked Arsenio.

'Hundred pesetas a sheep . . .'

'Sounds like a lot of money to me.'

107

'That's fourteen thousand seven hundred pesetas.'

Cash, it seemed, Arsenio could well understand. He counted out fifteen notes of a thousand and handed them to me.

'I'm sorry, I haven't any change.'

'Don't worry, we're all workers together. Heh, heh. We can let that slip or adjust the account next year: what do you say?'

'Well, fine. Thanks a lot.'

'What's he saying, Domingo?'

~

We stopped the car on the corner of the hill, a spot from where we could look down to the valley where we lived. Sitting in the deep grass we watched the hills change colour. 'My uncle screwed you,' said Domingo, sucking on a long stem of grass.

'How? It all seemed fine to me.'

'There were a hundred and fifty-one sheep.'

'How do you know?'

'I counted them this morning.'

'You might have made a mistake?'

'Impossible,' he replied with characteristic modesty. 'At lunchtime Pepe snuck into the stable and hid four shorn sheep in a little back room. He'd have hidden more if he hadn't seen me looking over the gate.'

'I can't believe they'd go to such trouble to save four hundred pesetas, and besides, he gave me three hundred pesetas on top of the money agreed.'

'That's the way my uncle is. He'll do anything to get the better of somebody; it doesn't matter who you are. That's why I told you to leave the pom-pom on the tip of the tails. That made him really wild. There's nothing a shepherd hates more than bits of wool left on his sheep. And he and Pepe are particularly sensitive about that.'

'I saw Pepe hacking away at the pom-poms with a pair of scissors as we left,' said Ana.

'Oh yes, they'll have to take them all off. They couldn't bear to have another shepherd see the flock looking like that. Hah, that really made them mad, that did!'

'So Arsenio has screwed us out of four hundred pesetas, but given me three hundred because I didn't have the change – that's one hundred profit . . . and we had a good lunch . . . '

'It was *regular* – alright.'

108

'*Regular* or not, I thought it was a good lunch, and most of his sheep have got ridiculous-looking pom-poms on their tails . . . so who's the winner today?'

'I think maybe we are today,' said Domingo with a grin, and we jumped up and walked back to the car. 'But watch out, because nobody ever gets the better of Arsenio, and he really is as bad as they come.'

~

From snippets I gathered from Domingo and his cousins over the following weeks, it seemed that my sheep-shearing trial had not gone badly. Nothing much was said, mind you, but the plain fact that none of the sheep had subsequently died took the wind from the sails of the luddite lobby, and messages of interest started to reach me from other shepherds. It was a heady endorsement, if a trifle low-key, and left me quite off my guard for the attack that was to come from another quarter.

Andrew, one of a small band of New Age travellers who had parked an ancient Bedford truck in our riverbed and was canvassing the local farms for work, saw the whole thing in a quite different light.

'There's something seriously wrong with your head, man, if you think it's okay to just come here and kill off all the old traditions with that machine of yours.'

The passion of this tirade amazed me. Andrew wasn't the sort to waste karmic energy on such an outburst. In fact he'd pared down his Mancunian brogue to the barest essentials necessary to accept a job, tell you whose round it was in the bar, and refuse food with meat in it. Besides, machines were his thing. For a whole day I had crouched next to him, passing him bits of assorted grease-covered metal while he tinkered beneath our Landrover.

109

'But this is progress,' I protested. 'Can't you see it benefits everybody?'

'Benefits you, maybe. What about the shepherds who come together to do the work, have a bit of a laugh and joke about it, get bevvied up, talk about the sheep, and that? What about their traditions? Gone down the pan, that's what.'

'Look, you've obviously never been near a sheep if you believe that drivel. Ask a shepherd if he fancies the prospect of a day's shearing and listen to what he says. Shearing is a pain and even if they do numb the pain with gallons of foul wine, it's no fun at all bending over bony, grubby sheep all day and snipping away with those ridiculous scissors they use to shear twenty or maybe thirty sheep. No, this is a good thing for the shepherds, and a lot easier on the poor sheep, too.'

Though I would never have admitted it to Andrew, I was not without qualms about the particular bit of progress I was spear-heading. For centuries the mountain shepherds had gathered, ten or twenty of them at a time, to shear together, and there was, as Andrew pointed out, a certain bonhomie to the occasion, with plenty of wine and a goat or lamb killed to finish the day. But there were also grease boils and huge blisters and swollen wrists and aching backs and the flies, dust and dung. The shepherds hated it and, from what Domingo had to say, couldn't do away with their social tradition fast enough.

110   The proof was that once I had demonstrated the efficacy of my machinery they started beating a path to my door – and, as you may have gathered, the path to my door is not even close to the route you might take on a stroll back from your local bar. It's a path that takes determined beating.

None of this, however, cut any mustard with the eco-funda-mentalists of Órgiva, who for months picked arguments with me about the havoc I was wreaking in the delicate balance between man and nature.

WALKING WITH THE WATER

ALONG THE CONTOUR LINES OF THE MOUNTAINS, A RIBBON OF bright green foliage delineates the *acequias* of the Alpujarras, an ancient system of irrigation channels that carry the rainwater and snowmelt from the high peaks to the valley farms. Debate smoulders as to whether it was the Romans two thousand years ago, or the Moors some eight hundred years later, who first built these channels. But whoever brought the idea here, it is, along with the terracing of the hills, the most important man-made element in the beauty of this landscape.

The principle behind this system of irrigation is simple: the rain and snow which falls in the huge catchment area of the mountains seeps down into vast aquifers or underground seams of water whence it is released slowly through the year to feed the rivers and springs which rise on the lower slopes. The *acequias* then channel off this water, carrying it at a gentle gradient down to the farms and villages below.

There is a lot of leakage involved but this is all part of the scheme of things. As the water runs along the channel it seeps through the earth and the cracks and the mole-holes to water the wild plants and the trees that grow along its banks. The root systems of these plants form mats that support the banks of the channels and stop them crumbling into the abyss below. Attempts to improve on nature by concreting parts of the *acequias* tend to do more harm than good. The plants bordering the channel dry up, the root system rots and loses its binding power, and the weight of the concrete and the water cause the whole thing to subside and distort the all-important levels.

There are literally hundreds of miles of *acequias* in the Alpujarras, and the paths along their banks, lined with grasses and a rich variety of alpine flowers – gentians, campanula, digitalis, saxifrage – make wonderful walking, with occasional heart-stopping views of the cirque of mountain peaks that rise to Veleta and Mulhacén. High in the mountains, way above the villages, the channels are wide streams of clear rushing water, ice-cold and, lying far above any possible source of contamination, delicious to drink. Lower down, where the *acequias* have their mouths in the valleys and gorges of the rivers, are dramatic stretches where the channels are cut into the rock of sheer cliff faces hundreds of feet high. These stretches were cut long ago with hammers and chisels by men suspended on ropes from the cliffs above.

112   In places the *acequias* flow along aqueducts mounted on walls of stone, built on hillsides too steep even to teeter on, let alone build a stone wall. The water rushes through tunnels full of bats and huge moths and out into the dazzling sunlight or on through shaded woods to plunge into impenetrable jungles of razor-edged leaves and thorny barbs.

Hundreds of small farmers depend on these *acequias* and so an organised social system has grown up to ensure an equitable

supply. Each *acequia* has its president, elected each year, its treasurer, and its *acequero*. The president presides over the democ-
ratic process of decision-making, resolves disputes and liaises
with the water authority. The treasurer takes the water-fees,
agreed upon every year by the waterers to cover costs of mainte-
nance and improvements. The *acequero* walks the full length of
the *acequia* every day and is responsible for its smooth running,
keeping an eye on leaks and danger points, and ensuring that
each waterer shuts his water off at the right moment without
running over into the next man's time.

If your land has water rights from a certain *acequia*, you are
allotted a certain time and a certain quantity of water. You may
be unlucky (or out of favour with the water president) and come
up with, say, seventeen minutes of one third of the *acequia* at ten
past three on Thursday mornings. Accordingly you plod out to
your orange grove and your vegetables with your torch stuck in
your mouth and your mattock over your shoulder. At ten past
three – not nine minutes nor eleven minutes past – you pull the
hatch and let the great body of water tumble through onto your
land. The *partidor*, a simple construction of bricks and mortar,
ensures that you only get a third of the water available.

If you don't have a tank in which to store your quota, you must
race frantically around in the dark, chopping with your mattock
at the little dams and dykes and channels, ensuring that each tree
gets a thorough soaking and every trench of vegetables fills to
the brim. On a night with a full moon this job can be a delight,
as ripples spread silver across the surface of the black water to an
accompaniment of trickling streams. But a tank is more practical and anyone with a little spare cash installs one so they can fill
it with their seventeen minutes of water and irrigate their land at
leisure the next day.

El Valero, standing alone on the far side of the river, is unusual

113

in that it has its own *acequia* – which is to say the potential for twenty-four hours of water seven days a week. There are no *acequia* dues to pay either, on the basis that if we want the water we have to clear the channels ourselves – a deal that struck me as very generous when it was first explained but which I've since come to have my doubts about. Pedro Romero had, predictably, been none too zealous in his duties as custodian of the El Valero *acequia*, although Maria, with occasional help from Bernardo, did what she could to coax a little more water to the farm through the silted-up channels, overgrown thickets and crumbling stone aqueducts.

When we first arrived to take possession of the farm, the *acequia* was in a dismal state. I almost despaired of ever getting it going again, as neighbours shook their heads and warned of its difficulties. Part of the problem is that it is entirely seasonal. Its mouth, a mile upriver from the farm, consists of a pool in the river, created by a makeshift dam of boulders and boughs, rusting sheets of corrugated iron and plastic sheeting. This gets swept away every year by the winter rains and has to be rebuilt every spring along with the cleaning of the channel.

The dam guides the water into the narrow mouth of the *acequia* where it begins a rapid descent down through a bed of red earth and through an alley of tall poplars. As the river drops away, it flows on across a scrub-covered hill, charting its course through tunnels of bramble, shallow grey bogs of reeds, and stretches of ground so barren that nothing will grow except capers. Finally, the water disappears into a tunnel beneath the farm's ancient threshing floor to emerge between the roots of an old fig tree, almost crystal clear, having deposited its red sludge along the channel.

From there it pours in a succession of cascades across a steep meadow known to us as Seven Scorpions (we tried to clear the field of stones just after we moved in, and under each of the first seven stones we lifted, we found a scorpion). Then, at last, it makes its way down along the edge of orange terraces and back into the river.

~

By the end of April, a distinct reluctance in the rainfall, and the feverish activity to be seen on the other *acequias*, alerted me to the necessity of getting some water through to the farm. As ever, I went across the river to see what Domingo had to say about the matter.

He was sitting on his *tinao*, or terrace, with his cousin Antonio and both were hacking away industriously with their knives, absorbed in the business of making little model ploughs. This was a rather odd notion that Domingo had hit upon to make a bit of money – a friend who ran a bar in the mountains had promised to display them on the wall and sell them. Tangles of copper wire, nuts and bolts and a big pot of varnish lay in disarray on the floor among the cats and the potatoes. Antonio's work station was supplied with a much depleted bottle of *costa* to which he was addressing himself with relish.

'It's his vice,' explained Domingo, blowing the shavings off a tiny wooden wedge he had just carved. 'He's no good without it . . . and he's not a lot of good with it either. Look at this, man! How the hell are you going to plough with a thing like that? Look here, it's twisted, it'll run off to the side . . . ' and he seized the model Antonio was working on and waved it disdainfully in the air towards me.

Antonio grinned good-naturedly and shook my hand. '*Encantado*,' he said in greeting, taking the tiny plough back from Domingo and placing it carefully on the pile of finished models.

'I can't see anyone's going to plough with it anyway, cousin – it's too damn small!' he added to Domingo as he drained down his glass of *costa*.

Eventually, I explained the reason for my visit to Domingo, who immediately volunteered his and Antonio's assistance – 'if he's sober' – in clearing my *acequia*, and suggested we start the next week.

I had my misgivings about the prospect of employing Antonio but there was little choice in the matter, and, in any case, my doubts proved unfounded. Antonio, even half-drunk, proved to be a man who worked with the capacity of a mechanical digger, and was cheerful with it, commenting on life in philosophical asides. The only problem was keeping him sober for more than a few days at a time, for, away from Domingo's watchful company, Antonio went on paralytic blinders of drinking.

When the two turned up, on the Monday morning agreed, Domingo gave me a stern warning about his cousin's contract of employment. 'Don't pay him anything,' he instructed. 'As soon as you give him money he'll be off and that'll be the last you or I will see of him.'

'But I've got to pay the bloke,' I protested. 'I can't let him work for nothing.'

'Well, save it up and pay him when the job's finished. And don't give it to him all in one lump either.'

116   It was kindly advice and with a hint of self-interest, too. Domingo told me how time and again he had found Antonio slumped in the gutter in one of the mountain villages, often badly cut from falling hard on the cobbles. He would haul him, soaked in wine and urine, into his car and take him down to La Colmena and nurse him back to some semblance of life. Antonio would return the favour, helping him with work around the farm. Then one day he'd be off, up early in the morning for the

four-hour climb up to his home village of Bubión, stopping on the way at Las Cañadillas to enjoy a litre or two of wine with another cousin who kept a few goats and liked to encourage Antonio in his habit.

∼

Domingo and Antonio turned up for the *acequia* task armed with picks, shovels, mattocks and sickles, and accompanied by two more *peones* – day labourers – Manolo, a young muleteer from the village with a mop of blue-black hair and a winning smile, and Paquito, whose dreamy look made me wonder if he was quite with us in this world. But they assured me that with a sickle in his hand he would perform in spectacular fashion.

We climbed the hill behind the house and dropped down into the *barranco* that leads to the tunnel. Paquito and Antonio pitched straight in with their sickles, clearing the overhanging mat of vegetation. I fought my way a few yards up the *acequia* to where there was a particularly nasty-looking patch of scrub. Grasping in my gloved hand a fistful of barbs and thorns, I hacked away with the sickle, entangling myself in a procession of hostile plants. First the brambles took hold of me, then the trumpet-vine, and as I was flailing about trying to extract myself from those fearsome tendrils, a pomegranate branch would bend forward and poke me in the eye, or a pampas grass would neatly slice into my neck. There wasn't a good-natured plant among the whole contorted tangle. I was getting nowhere, so I left the clearing and took up the shovel at the back of the gang.

Manolo and Paquito seemed to have no such problems with the jungle of plants and steadily disappeared into the distance, leaving the banks neatly trimmed behind them. Domingo and Antonio followed behind, clearing the silt and re-cutting the bed

117

of the channel, while I sweated and heaved at the back, shovel-
ling out the debris. With the exception of the shoveller, who
soon lost ground, the team moved along at an easy walking pace.

It was humbling to watch them. Every five minutes or so I
would straighten up to ease the agony in my back and wipe the
stinging sweat from my eyes; the others stayed down and just
kept on going. At the end of the day we ambled back along the
smooth hollowed ground to the farm. 'Have we really cleared all
this?' I wondered in disbelief as vista after vista of neatly opened
channel appeared around each bend like a well-manicured
woodland walk.

The second day was slower as we mulled over how we were
going to negotiate the dreadful stretch that ran below El
Avispero, an assault course of man-eating brambles and rubble-
strewn rockfalls. But somehow we got through it and towards
evening found ourselves easing through the softer earth and
gentler vegetation of the Barranco del Pino. By noon on the
third day we had emerged at the poplar alley below the dam.

There remained only the opening of the sluice to let the water
come pouring into the newly cleaned channel and work its way
down to our farm. Domingo calculated that it would take five
hours to get there, which left plenty of time to have lunch and
clear all the channels on the farm itself before it arrived. I was
delegated to walk with the water and see that the twigs and leaves
cut and fallen from the undergrowth didn't clog up the tunnels.

While other tasks sink into drudgery with constant repetition,
I never fail to delight in walking with the water. I sneak ahead of
its course and sit down to suck a stem of grass and contemplate
the peace, keeping an eye on the dry bed of the *acequia* and an
ear open for the gentle rustling of what is initially unrecognis-
able as water. It appears as a whispering mosaic of dried leaves,
petals, turdlets and twigs. Pink and white and golden, it creeps
quietly along, filling the hollows with a little rush and easing up

slowly to consume the high places. It was a thrill, that first day, watching as the water gathered and swelled and saturated the dry earth. It crept up the bank, pouring into the ant-hills and mole-runs, and little by little turned into a full-blown stream. Seeing it, I would splash through to the head and race around the next corner to await the miracle all over again.

~

Watering is a measure of manhood in the Alpujarras. A man who knows not the watering *no sirve* – he's useless. Domingo said to me one day in a fit of pique: 'You, Cristóbal, do not know the watering. You do not understand the water.' These were the harshest words he could have chosen, a vicious accusation impugning my worth. I think he had a hangover but the cut went straight to my heart. Wounded, I sat beneath a tree wondering about the watering. Maybe he was right. At the time of this attack I had been running the farm for only three years or so – no time to know the watering.

What I knew was that water had a tendency to run downhill, and when left to its own devices would always work its way to where you didn't want it, eroding terraces, destroying walls and exposing the roots of trees. If you saturated a terrace too much it could collapse with a noise like thunder, leaving a mess of tumbled earth and stones and trees on the terrace below, a disgrace that's difficult to hide and a lot of work to repair.

But when the watering goes well there's nothing quite like it. Building dams and channels of mud in the streams in the woods was my favourite occupation as a boy and I count myself lucky to be able to enjoy the same thing as an adult. In summer I water in rubber sandals, so while the rest of my body is burning, my feet and ankles are drenched in cool water. With my mattock I open the sluice in the main channel, moving the little dam of

119

earth and stones from the bank to the middle of the *acequia*. The brown swirling water brims over the side of the pool and then courses along the channels of the field and eases across the grass. Like a great amoeba the head of the water parts to go round the high spots, then slowly consumes them, darkening the pale dust before rejoining the stream. As the water reaches the trees and sinks to the roots, they seem to sigh, releasing clouds of scent.

I then wander about with my mattock adjusting the flow, tossing a stone into a too fast-flowing freshet, delivering a fierce chop with the mattock to increase a feeble flow. Eventually the distribution is nicely organised, with the water flowing just right to spread out and reach the bottom of the field in a few hours. Then along comes Beaune and flops down in the stream to cool off. The water, dammed by the dog, overflows the banks and messes the whole system up, so I have to start all over again. As evening falls, the swallows wing down from the houses and the rocks and skim above the water, wolfing the uncountable insects that cling to the tops of the grass-blades like sailors on the masts of sunken ships.

I love the watering and I'm hoping that by the time I've notched up twenty or thirty years' practice my neighbour might even admit that I know it.

CATS AND PIGEONS

'THE FIRST AND MOST IMPORTANT THING TO DO,' ANA
announced, looking decisively up from a book with a cat on the
cover, 'is to get those cats sorted out. We can't be surrounded by
creatures like that. It'll make us miserable. They must be reha-
bilitated.'

Besides a few rusting plant tins, the *camalas* and the brick,
Pedro had left us two cats. You don't move cats; they take root.
There was a starving husk of an old mother, and the feeble wisp
that was her offspring. The poor little creature had never had the
opportunity to be a kitten; it was born straight into a world of
hunger and blows. They were grey tabbies with much of their fur
scorched from seeking warmth in the hot ashes of the fire.

They slunk around, weak with hunger and worms, the picture
of dejection. Pedro hadn't cared much for his dogs – even his
three familiars, Tiger, Brown and Buffoon – but cats were
beyond consideration. They were allowed to attach themselves
to the house only because, according to Pedro, they were the

most fantastic ratters. It was hard to believe from the lifeless way in which they slouched about the place. Ana was right; their miserable plight was already getting to me.

Our initial task was to tame them so that we could get flea-collars over their heads and worm them. Ana is good with animals. It took about three days before they got the hang of being fed, and three days after that I found Ana stroking them on her lap.

We had thought that the business of the flea-collars would be all but impossible – feral creatures such as these would never accept such trappings of domesticity. In the event they both stood still and bowed their heads meekly to receive the collars. They almost seemed to know that this was a mark of being taken over by people who cared for them – or was that too foolish a notion? From there it was but a short step to a swift jab of wormer in the scruff of the neck.

Almost as we watched, the starveling creatures started a dim blooming. Their sunken sides filled out and their ribs disappeared, the scorched and patchy fur took on a lustre as some vestige of feline pride returned, and they even began to groom themselves.

Cats should have names and, for some reason best forgotten, these became Brenda and Elfine. Elfine, as her condition improved, started to develop what cat-lovers call 'personality'. One cat is much like another to me but I couldn't resist a sneaking affection for her. Brenda, the mother, was too far gone to bother much with personality development and remained something of an embarrassment to her more socially mobile offspring until one fateful day in the summer when a generous visitor was good enough to bring us a cold-bag full of smoked salmon. The mechanism of the cold-bag failed, or someone left the lid off in a hot car, with the result that the contents were declared to be 'suspicious'. Brenda died shortly afterwards of a surfeit of smoked salmon. Smoked salmon is, by a long head, my favourite food and I like to think that she departed this life with a gratified smacking of lips.

Elfine continued to thrive, and when she wasn't dozing she became, indeed, a great ratter. Or at least we think she did. The presence of rats and mice had been evidenced by their turds, little black pellets dotted about all over the house and terrace. Soon they disappeared altogether, which led us to one of two conclusions; either she was killing rats and mice very effectively or she was eating their turds.

∼

That spring and summer of our first year were stockpiled with projects. We had a home to rebuild and equip to modern tastes, an irrigation system to learn how to use, vegetables to nurture through to their first harvest, trees to prune, and fruit to pick. All of these were absorbing and necessary tasks and would have commanded our undivided attention had we not taken a walk along the riverbed one dewy morning and coincided with the weekly visit of the poultry man.

Every Saturday a large, cheerful-looking man in a big white van would turn up at first light at El Granadino, having driven all the way from Ciudad Real, three hundred kilometres distant. His van was equipped with special compartments stuffed full of every sort of poultry you could possibly desire: partridges, chickens of every description, ducks, geese and guinea-fowl, turkeys and quails, even peacocks. The first time we met him it brought a sort of poultry mania upon us. We drooled over the life-enhancing possibilities of these creatures that we could – for only a few pesetas – admit into our family orbit.

Returning home that night to give the dog and cat something to eat we were both struck by an indefinable feeling of loneli-

123

ness, as if the farm had become somehow depleted in our absence. Beaune and Elfine did the best they could. It simply wasn't their fault that they couldn't lay eggs.

The next Saturday we bought a couple of guinea-fowl and some quails and sped home, eager to introduce them to our circle. A few days later, Bernardo, moved by our poultry-keeping zeal, donated some chickens. Apparently they were rather special ones imported from Holland. They were fat and white and beautiful – for chickens that is – and the meat of them was said to be quite sublime. They were also supposed to lay eggs faster than you could count them.

'You've got a run prepared for them?' Bernardo asked.

'Yes,' I answered, thinking of the roughshod contraption I'd prepared in the stable below the house, 'all ready to go. But how shall I get them home?'

'We'll tie their feet together and make a loop in the string and you can carry them by that. How's that sound?'

'Alright,' I said, not altogether convinced.

'Right, ready? I'll go in and grab them and pass them out to you. Don't, whatever you do, let them go.'

Amidst a cacophonous cackling and squawking Bernardo insinuated his well-nourished frame through the tiny doorway of his chicken-run. He grabbed two, we tied them up, and I set off across the valley to the new Valero poultry-house.

124   It seems silly to be so sensitive in the matter of chickens but I found this method of transport rather barbaric. The confusion of the poor creatures as they sped along upside-down, heads just above ground level and feet pinched by the string, caused me distress. So I raced back across the valley with them, stumbling over stones, leaping over the rocks and hurtling across the uneven ground, keeping the chickens as steady and level as I could. Home I ran, alone in a grotesque egg-and-spoon race.

Arriving at El Valero, I scrabbled with the knots on the strings and feverishly loosed the cruel bonds. The chickens clucked and scuttled off into the shadows of their new home, quite unperturbed by the whole episode. I watched with pleasure as they made themselves at home, and then went to spend a pleasant hour delving in the 'eggs' chapters of my cookery books. 'Elizabeth David reckons there are 685 ways of dressing eggs in the French kitchen,' I announced.

The fever was truly upon us. Next to arrive were a couple of pairs of *palomas* – stock doves – which Old Man Domingo gave us. They arrived in a shoebox. In they went, into the stable beneath our bedroom where they gladdened our nights with their interminable clucking and shuffling and flapping and cooing. Old Man Domingo had said that it wouldn't take them long to get used to their new home.

'Just feed them inside for a few days, then open the hatch and let them go. They'll be back, you see if they aren't.'

So for a few days they joined in the chaos of our mixed bag of poultry, and then with trepidation we left their hatch open. Of course, nothing happened. However, after three days, they at last managed to find the hole, fluttered out and sat on the roof, blinking in the sunshine; a black one, a grey one and two white ones. They launched off into the plains of air above the valley, soaring and wheeling and stumbling in the currents with the unaccustomed use of their wings. Then they came back to sit on the roof and think about it, and then whoosh – off to do it again.

They were a wonderful sight. They really did seem to get as much pleasure from flying as I like to think I would. I spent hours watching them, nature's perfect complement to these little white farms high up on the sides of the valleys. But the next day a hurricane came, and as it thrashed and tattered the leaves of the eucalyptus and the ivy, it blew the poor little things away.

125

I was desolate. However, a few days later three of the birds limped back home from wherever the wind had blown them. The other had been eaten, we reckoned, by an eagle.

Pigeons are supposed to breed amazingly fast. Old Man Domingo had calculated that with the two pairs he'd given us we could expect over eighty squabs a year, and that they should start breeding within a month. But things didn't seem to work out quite as planned. We waited for weeks for one to go broody, watching eagerly for signs of amorous activity. It became apparent that the dark one, at least, was different from the others. Its two companions would sit together on the roof, while the dark one, who was slightly bigger, would sit some way off on its own and eye them up. Then it would sidle towards them nefariously, at which the two would jump off the roof.

'Do you suppose he's the male, Ana, and that this is what passes for an amorous advance in the pigeon world?'

'Yes, I'm pretty sure he's the male. But it doesn't look very promising, does it?'

Nonetheless, the male slowly began to get more insistent, and the females more compliant. This resulted in his jumping on them and pecking them ferociously in the back of the neck. It all looked rather unpleasant and we stopped observing them. However, some weeks later an egg was hatched and produced a live baby pigeon. This tiny creature was the first domestic animal born at El Valero during our time there – a poignant moment in its way. I was feeding the poultry and pigeons in the morning when I discovered a scrawny, damp little thing in the nesting box and raced up to tell Ana.

'Guess what? I think there's a baby pigeon at last!'

Ana was as excited as I was and dropped everything to come and investigate.

'It's no beauty, is it?' she commented. 'Do you suppose it really is a pigeon?'

126

'Well, its father's a pigeon, its mother's a pigeon, and there it is sitting in a pigeon's nest – I can't see what else it could be!'

'Maybe it's a cuckoo . . .'

Ana had a point. It was a most unprepossessing bird, blackish-brown with tatty feathers and very peculiar proportions as to the head and body. It was hard to believe that it could have sprung from the egg of such a pretty creature as a pigeon.

'No. Cuckoos lay their eggs in nests in the wild – not in stables. I think it is a pigeon.'

～

It was indeed. It had taken about three months for our pigeon population to increase from four . . . to four. I began to see Old Man Domingo's forecasts as an optimistic target. At this rate we would be lucky to dine on one pigeon pie a year. In fact, it began to dawn on us that the poultry department as a whole was failing to thrive. We were putting in a fair quantity of the recommended input but there didn't seem to be much output at all. A general reluctance to breed or increase or grow, or even to lay eggs, had taken over. Clearly something was amiss. We did some observing, and some thinking, and came to the conclusion that it was mutual antipathy that was affecting performance.

The quails, the smallest of the menagerie, were frightened of the chickens; the chickens didn't like the guinea-fowl or the pigeons, though they could live with the quails; the guinea-fowl were indifferent to the pigeons but were terrified of the quails and hated the chickens; the pigeons were affected by the guinea-fowls' terror of the quails, nervous of the possibility of a chicken –quail alliance, piqued by the indifference of the guinea-fowl, and shared everybody else's dislike of the chickens.

It wouldn't do; action needed to be taken. So we designed and built a contraption that came to be known as the Quail

127

Recreation Facility – QRF for short. If we could get the quails out of the equation we might be able to make some sense out of the rest of it all.

We consulted a number of works on the subject and slowly a design appeared. The three factors we had to bear in mind in the construction were happiness, security and portability. In order to get maximum performance from our quails we decided that we needed to simulate, as far as possible within the confines of a wired-in box, the conditions they enjoyed in the wild.

We came up with a sort of portable ark with an enclosed nesting-box and night-quarters at one end, served by a cunningly contrived trapdoor. The other end was wired in, but the bottom was open to allow the incumbents access to whatever piece of ground the thing was standing on. A mesh skirt, weighted down with stones, surrounded the outside area. The finished thing seemed to me to be the very acme of modern, enlightened poultry-keeping.

The quails, sadly, had other ideas. When we introduced them to their new home, they beetled straight into a corner of the nesting-box and there lurked disconsolate and depressed. Then after a week or so of this unpromising behaviour they at last managed to experience one of the few conditions that quails enjoy in the wild, that of being eaten by a fox.

The removal of the quails was insufficient to settle the disharmony in the poultry-house. The cross-currents of mutual antipathy continued to affect performance. So we prepared an appealing home for the hated chickens, an attractive, traditionally built stone chicken-shed with spacious outside recreation area and fox-proof door. In went the chickens and shortly afterwards we were thrilled to be presented with our first egg.

I gave the egg full culinary attention according to the French manner as retailed by Elizabeth David. First I plunged it in fiercely boiling water for a minute, then I took the pan off the heat and left it there for a further five minutes, then I rinsed it with cold water, and ate it. It was like no other egg I've ever eaten, done to exquisite perfection.

Unfortunately, as I was eating the egg, a stoat or a weasel was eating the chickens. And it was not very many weeks later that first the guinea-fowl and then the pigeons went the way of the others. Foxes, snakes, stoats, weasels, martens, wild cats, rats, were all lying in wait to discourage any move we made in the direction of poultry-keeping. Our skills and our facilities were not up to their onslaughts. However we tried to mend and patch the walls and wires of our poultry-places, the creatures of the wild outwitted us.

Reluctantly, we gave up the project. We had too many other tasks bearing down on us – not least the rebuilding of our own home – to spend any more time feeding fresh fowl to visiting predators. I consoled myself with the thought that this was only our first attempt. There'd be other chances to get it right and become the proud owners of the sort of happy and secure poultry-yard that you find in children's books.

BUILDING THE HOUSE

FOR SOME MONTHS A STOCKPILE OF CHESTNUT ROOF-BEAMS had lain under a tarpaulin on a piece of flat land behind the house. It was a reminder to us of urgent work ahead, yet neither of us could summon up enthusiasm to get started. The leaks Domingo had forecast with the spring rains had not been so bad and placing a few buckets in strategic positions seemed a much easier solution than the wholesale dismantling of our home.

As summer arrived, however, a new problem presented itself, and one that finally goaded us into action. The hosts of creatures that had moved into the cane and brush ceiling in our bedroom began to breed and multiply, scuffling and skittering not six feet above our upturned and tremulously wakeful faces. As the heat of the night increased, the breeding and multiplying above us became ever more frenzied, and soon, as the population soared out of control, we found ourselves spattered with larvae, maggots and other young deemed surplus to requirements. This was hardly conducive to a good night's rest. The roof would have to go. And while we were about it, we argued, we might as well make a few small adjustments to our living space.

Since moving into El Valero we had billeted ourselves in the larger of the two stone buildings. This stood on a steeper part of the rock with its *tinao*, or covered terrace, looking out across a wide sweep of the gorge with the rivers snaking below. To one side was the bedroom and to the other a small, windowless box of a room that passed for the kitchen, the surprisingly appointed shower room, and another long narrow room which shared the same fine views as the terrace and bedroom but had no glass in the windows. This rather limited its function as a sitting room and on inclement days, when we were forced off the *tinao*, there was little to do but sit disconsolately on our bed and stare out of the window.

Pedro's old quarters, just below and to the east, were of humbler design and in much worse repair. They consisted of two interconnecting rooms: his kitchen with its hearth, and the dark, airless storeroom where he housed his hams, his tools and his bed. We hadn't yet found a use for these rooms so we decided that they would be the best place to begin rebuilding work. If we knocked out the internal wall and added an L-shaped extension we could create a living room large enough to spread out our worldly encumbrances, and a kitchen for all weathers. Once we'd moved in we could start work on the rest.

Even in the wilder wilds of Spain you need permission to start tampering with external walls so I went to open negotiations with the town hall. Within the week a municipal policeman was dispatched to make the necessary investigations. He arrived on foot one hot May morning, the heat and dust of the valley having made no obvious impression on his impeccable uniform. His shoes still shone, his shirt remained perfectly pressed, and he positively bristled with authority and efficiency. We offered him coffee as a restorative and he told us that if ever we needed a

131

friend in high places then he was our man. We were very impressed.

'So it's just one storey then, is it?' he asked settling down to business. We described what we had in mind.

'And you're not going to use any asbestos in the construction?' We assured him the idea was abhorrent to us.

'Well then,' he said, handing the coffee cup back for a refill, 'you'll be alright. You can do as you please.'

With the bureaucratic obstacles out of the way there seemed nothing to prevent our getting on with the work . . . except that I hadn't a clue how to go about it. In my former life handyman-ism had been hateful to me. I was the sort of man who would baulk at putting a hook on a door, preferring to wait until some-one happened along with the tools and talent for the job. At El Valero it was all going to be different. I would have to do things for myself. I looked around for some simple task that I could tackle as a way of easing myself into my new role as builder and site manager.

The stone walls of the little house were stuck together with mud, and much of the mud seemed to be falling out. Repointing the walls seemed rudimentary enough. On my next trip to Órgiva I bought a couple of sacks of cement, a heap of sand and a trowel. With a little hand-pick I scraped as much mud as I could from the joints between the stones and then set to with the trowel, refilling the cavities with a strong mix of sand and cement. It was satisfying in a tedious sort of a way, but it took me nearly a week to finish one stretch of about ten metres.

Just as I was stepping back to admire my work Domingo appeared.

'I'm repointing this wall,' I told him brightly.

He looked at the finished section through narrowed eyes as he sucked on a stem of grass.

'What do you think, then?'

He shook his head and walked over to run his hand along the surface.

'It's twisted,' he announced.

'What's twisted?'

'The whole wall is twisted.'

'So?'

'It'll have to come down . . . if you want, I'll come over and give you a hand.'

⌒

Two days later Domingo arrived with tools and trestles and a set of straight-edges that he had just had made up in town. 'Right,' he said, 'first we'll take the roof off, then we'll knock the wall down.' And he pitched into the work like a wrecking machine. By the afternoon of the first day we found ourselves standing on a pile of rubble where a tolerably good and rather pretty house had stood a few hours earlier.

Were it not for my steadfast faith in the skills of Domingo I might have curled up and wept. But I knew I would enjoy the work ahead with my mentor-neighbour. Not that Domingo was a sensitive teacher; the idea wouldn't have occurred to him. If I laid a stone that did not conform to his idea of the correct *postura* he would shout at me. 'No!! Not like that. Dick in vinegar, man! If you lay them like that the wall will be shit, and when we come to put the roof on it'll fall down.' Then he would stump around to my side of the wall, grab the offending stone and thump it down so that it sat correctly.

'Ah, like that you mean . . .'

Building in stone is a very inexact science. Each stone has seven *posturas*, local wisdom has it, and none of them is ever exactly right for where you want the stone to be. So the placing of each stone is a compromise and over each one a taxing decision must

133

be made. It's very wearing on the mind, but there is a tremendous satisfaction in seeing a wall rising steadily from the ground, as if by organic extension of the soil itself.

Little by little I learned, and Domingo was able to spend less time shouting at me and more placing his own stones. My job was to mix the cement and lay the inside of the walls, while Domingo saw to the more important outside facing. He seemed to be very good at it and in not too many days we stood back to admire a straight and imposing piece of masonry the very size, girth and essence of a wall.

'Where did you learn to build in stone like this?' I asked. 'It's beautiful.'

'Why, here, working with you,' he replied, as if surprised by the implication that he had ever wielded a trowel before. But he'd often seen it done, he hastened to assure me.

In the event it didn't seem to matter that we were two entire novices. Domingo's unshakeable self-confidence infected me, and within a couple of weeks we were both cocky and halfway competent builders. The architectural side of things we dealt with on pieces of scrap paper with a biro and a tape measure. Domingo had all sorts of fanciful notions of long-beamed porticos and stone pillars and arches, but I reckoned his plans were a little too ambitious for our humble mountain home.

134   ∾

We took a break before starting work on the extension walls where the new kitchen was to be sited. Domingo had fallen behind with his farmwork and I too needed to catch up on tasks left undone. But then on the day we were due to restart, Domingo failed to turn up. I humped a few stones about on my own but made so little progress it seemed a waste of time. He didn't turn up the day after either. When I finally found him he seemed troubled.

'What happened to you on Monday?'

'I was in hospital in Granada. My mother's been taken ill.'

'What's wrong with her?'

'Cancer of the kidneys. They say she won't last more than a couple of weeks.' The last words were stifled in an attempt to prevent the tears breaking through.

I stared back appalled. This couldn't be true. Expira was so healthy, such a solid, comfortable presence. How could she be dying? Domingo, in defeated tones that were heartwrenching to hear, told me a few sketchy details about Expira's mysterious pains and an emergency referral from the doctor's surgery. I groped around for some words of comfort and reassurance but there was nothing I could find in either language that came even close to the mark. Expira would have known what to say, but Expira was in hospital.

The thought prompted me to be practical. I arranged to go over and feed his livestock for him before taking some food and a few extra toiletries to the hospital the next day. Then I went back to break the news to Ana.

~

The next morning we met Domingo in the bar of the Hospital of the Virgin of the Snows. He had black bags beneath his eyes and had obviously been weeping.

'All my mother's relatives have come down from Barcelona and Zaragoza,' he told us. 'And all her sisters from the Alpujarra. They're here, waiting . . .

'They say it won't be long now,' he added quietly, as we trudged forlornly along the broad hospital corridors. As we approached

135

Expira's ward the corridor seemed to fill with black-clad figures. They were bent in attitudes of unutterable dejection; some of the old women keened quietly as they rocked to and fro. The men stood with their hands in their pockets looking down at the lino floor and wondering what to say. Some children were trying hard to play through the thickening atmosphere of gloom. 'Shsshh!' their parents admonished them.

Old Man Domingo was there, rocking quietly back and forth, his eyes downcast. We shook hands and mumbled . . . I didn't know what condolences were in Spanish – only felicitations.

Then Domingo ushered us through the swing-doors and over to Expira's bed. She was propped up against a huge pillow and, startlingly, she looked absolutely radiant. In fact, I'd never seen her looking so well. Perhaps it was partly the contrast of her tanned face against the white of the hospital nightgown and sheets. I wasn't used to seeing Expira clad in white. But nonetheless, this was not the deathbed scene I had dreaded.

Expira dissolved into a huge smile and embraced us warmly. 'Ay, how wonderful to see a couple of cheerful faces! Everybody here is so gloomy it makes me feel miserable. I wish they'd just clear off and leave me in peace but they won't. They just hang around getting glummer and glummer.'

We gave her the bags of grapes and peaches that we'd brought along for her. 'Well, you look pretty good to me, Expira – you look wonderful,' I said.

'And I feel fine too. I'm having a good rest. It hurts me a bit here, mostly when I laugh, but with all these muttonheads around me I don't get much chance of that.' She indicated the members of her extended family peering round the door.

We sat on her bed, one on either side, and did what we could to bring a little cheer to what Domingo reckoned were his mother's last few days.

136

Later, as we left the hospital, he explained. 'They're going to operate on Friday on the growth on her kidney, but even if it's successful it will only give her another week or so, another week of pain and misery.'

'She doesn't look that miserable to me, Domingo. She looks better than I've seen her for a long time. Are you quite sure about this?'

'It's what the doctor told us.'

We didn't know what to think. We'd both been deeply upset at the news of Expira's illness and its desperate prognosis, but felt our hearts lightened by the state in which we'd seen her.

'She certainly doesn't look like a dying woman to me,' said Ana emphatically.

∼

On Saturday morning I went across to La Colmena to see Domingo. He would break his vigil every day to come home and feed the chickens and rabbits and partridges and pigs. I found him whistling as he poked food through the bars of the tiny cage where an unfortunate male partridge lived out its miserable existence.

'How did the operation go?'

He turned around and grinned a grin I hadn't seen for a long time. 'She's alright. Much better. It wasn't cancer at all.'

Apparently, at the end of the operation, while all the family were keeping tearful vigil outside the theatre, the doors suddenly flew open and a doctor burst out beaming. It wasn't cancer at all, just a stone in the kidneys. There was no danger. Expira would spend a day or two in the hospital recovering from the operation, then she could go home.

Of course there was much rejoicing at Expira's miracle, but

137

Domingo and his father had had a serious shock. Things could never go back to being quite the way they were before Expira's hospitalisation. As if by magic they gathered all their apparently scant resources and bought a flat in town – for cash. Expira needed rest from the relentless labour of running a *cortijo* and looking after the men in her family, and Domingo was determined that she should get it. The flat was immediately furnished with a freezer, a washing-machine and a huge TV whose colour system offered pictures in tones of red or green.

Expira and Old Man Domingo treated the flat with suspicion. We went to see it, and the radiant and newly recovered Expira showed us proudly around, pointing out the more impressive features: the chandelier – *sine qua non* of all modern Spanish homes (and especially the poorest), and the bathroom with all its myriad methods of dispensing miraculous running water. 'It tastes disgusting – filthy water, you can't drink it,' said Expira laughing happily.

Old Man Domingo extricated himself from the leatherette sofa, where he had been sitting mesmerised in a detached sort of a way by the nonsense that was unfolding in shades of iridescent green on the telly. 'Come,' he beckoned, and led us outside to his domain. Beyond the flat's kitchen door was a patch of land the size of a bedsheet – already laying claim as the most intensive patch of cultivation in Europe. There was once a fashion for writing postcards with the writing crossing in two directions, in order I suppose to get more on the card. This was just what Old Man Domingo had done with his plot.

'Look,' he said, proudly. 'Here are the aubergines and the tomatoes and do you not see the little peppers?'

Indeed we did, crammed tightly into their lovingly prepared ridges and furrows, criss-crossed by the young aubergines and the little tomatoes already tied to their first step up the canes.

138

The Meleros were not thinking of living permanently in the flat, it was just a bolt-hole for when things got too rough out at the *cortijo*, somewhere Expira could take things a little easier, but nevertheless the priority was to get the vegetables in.

We sat on the sofa and drank a glass of wine.

'Life in the *cortijo* is hard,' said Expira. 'All that dust and dirt and the flies and the wretched animals, and here it's easy – why, four strokes of the broom and the place is spotless. But there's nothing to do except sit and look at that horrible television. There isn't even a view to make you happy,' she declared, pointing through the window at the wall of the next block of flats. 'You couldn't live here long or you'd go crazy.'

~

In the new circumstances of his mother's close encounter with the glory and her convalescence in town, Domingo couldn't spare much time for the building work at El Valero. He had too much work of his own to do and in any case, he explained, I knew the business well enough by now to carry on by myself.

I had indeed learned both techniques and confidence from Domingo's idiosyncratic tuition, and perhaps he was right, maybe I could rebuild a house alone. But building a stone house on your own is a job that would take for ever. I needed help. As luck would have it, help wasn't too far off.

An hour's walk up the Cádiar river lies Puerto Jubiley, a tiny, more or less abandoned village that straddles the river just before it enters the gorge. Ana and I used to walk up there every now and then to give the dog an airing. The shade cast by the steep cliffs and the swiftly flowing water cool the air in the gorge so on a hot night it is like walking up a cool river of air. Because few people use the river-path these days, the wild creatures that

139

inhabit the cliffs and hills come down without fear to the water to drink. You are almost certain to see ibex, boar or eagles, or just water-snakes, frogs, turtles and lizards.

One evening, Ana and I were taking a walk through the small riverside *vega* of neatly cultivated maize and alfalfa fields that form a bright patchwork of green among the canebreaks at the border of the outlying ruins of the village. A couple stood squinting suspiciously into the evening sun at us from the front of one of the first of the tumble-down houses.

'*Hola, buenas tardes*,' we said, returning their suspicious look. They didn't look anything like our idea of Spanish villagers, too fair, too obviously . . . English.

'*Buenas tardes*,' they replied. 'You don't look Spanish at all.'

Cathy and John turned out to be long-term refugees from English life, having moved to Spain a decade earlier and, after living for a couple of years near Seville, settled upon this remote spot. On that first meeting – tea followed by wine – we all found ourselves resenting our shared Englishness. After all, we were more or less next-door neighbours and none of us had come to Spain to live next door to our compatriots.

Still, it wasn't long before we forgave each other's origins and a friendship developed. Cathy and John lived in circumstances like our own, and were also doing up their ramshackle village house bit by bit, with the limited sums of money they earned through teaching English, doing building work and carpentry, and acting as guides through the arcane web of Spanish administration for other foreigners buying property in the area.

We hit upon a work-exchange arrangement together. Once a week I would ride up to the Puerto and spend a day labouring on our new friends' house, retailing the information I had picked up from Domingo's building lessons. And in return we had the benefit of John and Cathy's skills in plumbing, electrics, plastering and carpentry. At El Valero, tasks with pipes which had before seemed fantastically complex were painlessly completed. An electrical system was installed to work off the new solar panels I had bought in Granada, and little by little the house shed its peasant rags and started to move into what remained of the twentieth century.

However, with just the three of us working sporadically, and with occasional help from Ana, progress was pathetically slow. I couldn't see us getting the house finished in less than a couple of years. We had to take some action to speed things along. So at the instigation of Carole, my level-headed sister in London, I placed an advertisement in New Zealand House to see if I could persuade some itinerant Kiwis to lend a hand. They would be offered a laughable pay-packet but a chance to see a bit of Andalucía, eat a lot of home cooked food and drink as much *costa* as they dared. I had worked with New Zealanders in fencing and shearing gangs in Britain and admired their easygoing cheerfulness and propensity for enjoying hard work.

We got more than seventy-five replies. Carole shortlisted them and conducted interviews using a checklist that I had supplied her with. Then I did the final interviews myself from the phone office in Órgiva.

∾

So we found ourselves once again in company at El Valero, living with four strong Kiwis: David and Gitte, Keith and Diane. I took over Domingo's role and laid the all-important outside stones while shouting at the others till they got their stones right. The system worked well and before long, with the benefit of all the talents and skills of the team, plus Cathy and John's groundwork, the house started to take shape.

'Spontaneous Architecture,' Keith called it. He had trained as an architectural draughtsman in New Zealand and was initially horrified by the way we flouted conventional design procedures. The height of the risers of the patio stairs, for example, was governed by the size of the stones we were using to build them, and almost everything else was likewise designed to fit the materials to hand. Water-pipes were left exposed and electric cables were run along the surface of the walls, rather than being needlessly chased into the stone.

It took about five months to complete the house, with the stone floors laid, the new chestnut beams hoisted into position, and cleaned and oiled with the requisite twelve coats of linseed oil, the plumbing all set to go, and all the rustic woodwork neatly scarfed together. The centrepiece was an elegant fireplace with a moulded chimney and a curved olive lintel, built to the specifications of one Count Rumford, an enthusiast for open fires who had experimented with hearth designs in the late nineteenth century in America. He had come up with the perfect proportions to get the smoke away and up the chimney and the heat out into the room. Our homespun version of the same was a joy to behold.

We had a celebration dinner to admire the finished work – a 'roof-shout' the Kiwis called it. Cathy and John had thoughtfully provided some champagne and in the glow of bonhomie that such bottles produce, Keith announced that he and Diane were going to use our Spontaneous Architectural principles on the house they planned to build in New Zealand.

142   Then a hush descended as I stooped to light the great stack of rosemary and olive logs that we had laid in the grate. The little flame from the match leapt into the kindling and in seconds became a blazing roar that boomed in the chimney, illuminating the room with a dancing ruddy glow. I couldn't help but feel a little weepy. It was almost as if I was setting in motion the heart of our new home.

DOGS AND SHEEP

AS AUTUMN MOVED INTO WINTER, SNOW FELL IN THE HIGH
sierra and the olives turned through purple to shiny black on
the trees. It rained and the countryside started to look a little
greener, the plants less withered and dusty. Following the example of our neighbours, we set to work harvesting our first olive
crop, beating down the ripe fruit with long canes and gathering
them in nets spread beneath the trees.

A proper olive-picker will beat every last fruit from the tree,
risking life and limb if necessary to creep out along a flimsy
branch and whop a single recalcitrant olive. We weren't up to
such exacting standards and risked losing respect by leaving several kilos dangling from the more awkward branches. One of the
fortunate things, however, about living in a remote spot like El
Valero is that few people pass by and you can get away with the
odd bit of botching.

By the time we had got round all of the trees we had picked
about five hundred kilos, which we sacked up, separating out

all the leaves and twigs, heaved onto the Landrover, and drove to the mill in Bayacas. This is one of the few mills where they press the olives cold, which gives a much better quality of oil. The rate is about four to one, that is to say, you get a litre of oil for every four kilos of olives you deliver. A hundred and twenty litres would be enough for a year's supply with plenty left over to present to our less agriculturally-minded friends. This was our first stab at self-sufficiency and we couldn't help but feel a little smug about the results.

By December the snow line had crept round to the peaks of the Contraviesa to the south, clipping the southern wind with an icy chill. The farmwork had settled into a lull and Ana and I were casting about for other projects. Bonka came bounding to the top of our list. She was a sheepdog puppy owned by some English friends of ours who live on a hillside surrounded by almond trees above the Río Chico. They were looking for homes for their new litter of puppies and as we'd always admired the affectionate mother, and were keen to find a companion for Beaune, we decided to stop off and look them over.

Bonka was the obvious choice, and swiftly named (Ana insists that all her dogs begin with B) after a brand of coffee. She bore the closest resemblance to her mother, and seemed to have inherited her calm, playful manner. She also had paws like shovels, promising to match her mother for size. Most endearing of all, however, was her bark. For some reason Bonka's bark sounded uncannily like a dog trying to impersonate a duck, an impression that grew stronger the more menacing she tried to sound. As far as we knew this was a unique ability in the dog world and not to be overlooked when considering the future matriarch of El Valero's pups. Beaune, sadly, had been neutered when young and could do little to further the line herself.

Bonka ingratiated herself easily with Beaune and soon made

144

herself at home with the other inhabitants of the farm. We were amazed how quickly she seemed to slot in. One day, however, she came haring into the house with her tail between her legs, whimpering in terror. Some strange new experience had proved too frightening for her. I went outside to investigate. The hillside above the house was awash with sheep. It was the flock of Geraldo, a young shepherd who grazed the high eastern Alpujarra, round the villages of Nieles and Juviles. Every winter he would come down to pasture his flock for a month in the almond groves of the Venta del Enjambre following the Via Pecuaria, an ancient droveway, that runs straight through our farm.

I watched as the main flock scuffed down the track. They were a pretty unprepossessing bunch, being on the thin side and scraggy with it, with a pronounced tendency towards the goat in them. Yet, as they dropped out of sight into the tamarisk woods by the river, leaving an unmistakable miasma in their wake, I found myself lost in covetous thoughts. A decision that I had delayed making began to resolve itself and press for action. The time had come to buy some sheep of my own.

Ana had reservations about sinking most of our remaining savings into sheep-rearing, and reminded me that our sheep enterprises in Britain had hardly succeeded in making us rich or even comfortable. It was a fair comment but one that pitifully overlooked the existential nub of the matter. I pointed out how essential livestock were to a farm; that it was a travesty to even call El Valero a farm, or expect us to be taken seriously as the owners of it, when we only had a couple of dogs and cats in residence. Surely also she didn't want to let her skills as a stockwoman go to waste?

Then, embellishing freely, I depicted how trim the farm would look with sheep nibbling away at all the thickets and encroaching creepers and clipping considerably the overgrowth that

145

threatened our paths. This last thought seemed to sway her just a little. I could tell that with some more skilful persuasion, she could be brought round to my way of thinking.

∼

The Sierra de Segura is a rather bleak range of high mountains four hours' drive away in the north of Granada province. The hub of the area is the small agricultural town of Huescar, a modest place callously omitted from every guidebook that I've ever consulted, but the home, nonetheless, of the exalted *Asociación Nacional de los Criadores de la Oveja Segureña* – ANCOS – the Segureña sheep society.

I hadn't actually seen a Segureña sheep in the flesh but I had seen them portrayed on a chart in the agricultural office in Órgiva. Their carriage and conformation were quintessentially ovine and the wool was white and, well . . . woolly. They looked so superior that I was convinced they were the stock for El Valero. Anxious not to let the side down as a fellow farmer and breeder, I polished my shoes, put on a white shirt, shaved, and fished out the only pair of jeans that I own with no holes in them. Then, on a chill December afternoon, I removed some cash from the bank and headed north from Granada.

It was evening when I arrived in Huescar and its streets were empty. The whole population, it seemed, were either out in the fields or huddled around *braseros* – small coal stoves that are fitted under the table – in their homes. As I had no idea how to find the ANCOS office, I slipped into a bar. There was only one other customer.

I ordered a drink and asked the bartender for directions. 'Toñito!' he called to the other customer far down the bar in the shadows. 'This gentleman is looking for ANCOS. You know where it is, don't you?'

146

At this signal Toñito slithered along the bar towards me, burbling and dribbling as he came. I looked to my clean shirt with
misgivings. 'Good evening, Antonio,' I greeted him. 'I am told
you know where I might find the offices of ANCOS.'

'Pah!' he spat. 'I know where to find ANCOS and all the other
cabrones you might wish to find. But first we must take a few
drinks together, eh?'

Why is it that I so often seem to find myself in this ridiculous
situation? Other men manage to enter and leave bars without
having to spend whole evenings entertaining the local drunk.
But for some reason big-talking boozers unfailingly zero in on
me, sniffing perhaps a foolish politeness, a wish not to offend a
stranger in a strange town.

Anyway, of all the many local drunks I've had the misfortune
to attract, Antonio was the dregs of the barrel. One drink followed another and another until I despaired of completing my
mission and resigned myself to remaining a drinking hostage for
the rest of the night. Then all of a sudden he swung to his feet,
announced that he would now take me to ANCOS and lurched
out of the bar hauling me along by the arm. I could have wished
for a better guide than this man who was staggering ahead of
me, slobbering and howling obscenities as he went, but there was
no other choice and he at least knew the way.

'Where are you from, my friend? I can see you are not one of
us?' We had already covered this ground in the bar but repeti-
tions seemed not to bother him.

'I'm English actually.'

'And from where would that be?'

'England.'

'Ah England, yes . . . I am well known in that land . . . perhaps
you know Fernando Jiménez . . ? ' He shot me a quizzical look.

'No . . . I don't think so. I couldn't be sure. Where in England
would Fernando Jiménez live now?'

'Barcelona.'

'Ah, now there you are mistaken, my friend, for Barcelona is not in England, it is in the north of Spain . . .'

'No, Fernando lives in England – Barcelona, England.'

Thus we progressed towards the offices and waiting worthies of ANCOS. I wanted to cut short this conversation about the location of Barcelona – it wasn't getting us anywhere – but introducing another topic seemed somehow reckless. Toñito, however, had no such reservations.

'Did you see the football?'

'No. I don't actually have a television . . .'

'Then you'd have seen the goal in the second half . . .'

'I didn't see the match, man!'

'You couldn't have missed it – Fernando Jiménez . . .'

'Surely not the same Fernando Jiménez who . . .'

But we had arrived outside the offices of ANCOS.

'Well, my friend, thank you very much for . . .'

'Wait. I am known here. I'll get Pedro for you.'

'Really, please, I wouldn't want to put you to the trouble.'

'No, no, it's no trouble.'

He stood on the opposite pavement and yelled up at the first-floor window.

'Pedro! Pedro Gallego, you son of a whore!'

There was no reply. I considered bolting.

'Pedro! Pedro, are you deaf, you pox-spotted shit? I shit on your dead, man – can't you hear me?'

Toñito stooped to pick up a stone and hurled it at the window. The fates had not at least deserted me altogether. The stone crashed into the frame.

'Pedro, you Black Milk! Dick in vinegar, where are you, man?'

The window flew open and a face appeared. The face considered us without enthusiasm. I smiled, made a little bow and attempted to introduce myself. Toñito shouted me down.

148

'I've brought someone to see you, Pedro. He wants some sheep. I shit on your sheep!' And so saying, he lurched off down the street.

~

It wasn't the most promising start but I'd forgotten the whole episode within a couple of hours, as I found myself dining with Pedro Gallego and his family and friends. We ate among other things the delicious cêpes of the Sierra de Segura, seared in butter and then simmered in wine and herbs. After the meal, the men, who had done most of the cooking, washed up, while the women dandled the babies. This was modern Spain.

The next day I set out with Pedro and his father, Don Antonio. Pedro was the secretary of ANCOS; his father, a real Spanish grandee, passionate about sheep, was the president. We clattered around the mountain tracks all morning, visiting farms and looking at beautiful ewe-lambs in stables deep with bright straw bedding.

We eventually selected twenty-five lambs, a dozen in-lamb ewes, and a ram-lamb. I paid a very fair price for them and we organised a lorry to bring them to Órgiva a few weeks later. Then we repaired to a bar to refresh ourselves.

Don Antonio rejected a good-looking seafood *tapa*.

'Take that muck away, boy, and give us a proper *tapa* of Segureña sheepmeat.'

'Yes sir,' said the boy.

~

By the end of December, the river had swollen with the winter rain. The rickety old footbridge that had served us since we came was listing badly to one side and the bits of driftwood that com-

149

prised its walkway were either broken or gone, leaving intimidating gaps. Crossing the bridge was disconcerting enough for Ana and me, well practised in the art, and we had the new flock to think of. There was no way that I would be able to coax such skittery creatures onto such a flimsy contraption. The bridge needed rebuilding. I discussed the problem with Domingo. He had an idea about a quick and easy way to get the job done.

On New Year's Day Domingo killed his pigs. After the midday feasting he suggested to the dozen or so men who had come to the *matanza* that they should help me rebuild my bridge. Not everyone fancied the prospect of splashing around in icy water but he was persuasive. It would be in their interests to do so, indeed it was even their obligation as owners of land on the far side of the river. It would also be a good way to dispel the boozy torpor that held them all in its grip.

'The trouble with all these slobs,' he complained, 'is that they've lost the habit of building bridges. Before, when it rained properly, we had to build a new bridge at least four or five times a year. We used to be pretty good at it.'

We trooped down the hill to the river and looked at the sad collection of poles and driftwood that spanned it. Of all the company I was the only one who had never before built a bridge. Everyone else knew exactly how it was done. They knew how big it should be, what it should be made of, and, most importantly, where to put it. Unfortunately, building homespun bridges is not an exact science, and thus no two men's notions coincided exactly. Frasco, who had had a lot of experience, being the eldest present, said that we should forget about Romero's lethal jumble of wood and build a new one just downriver from the track, where we could anchor the beams to a giant eucalyptus.

'You're talking silly, man!' said Domingo. 'You can't possibly build it there; the ground is soft and as soon as the river gets up it'll wash it away.'

'This is the spot,' said José, stamping the ground a few metres upriver of the old bridge. 'It's the narrowest point and the ground's good and solid.'

'Solid – the Host! If you build it there it'll be swept away in days. There's never been a bridge there.'

'Yes, it must be upstream, over there by the oleander – there the river won't move . . .'

'No, the most important thing is to take advantage of that boulder and use it as a pier, that way we'll . . .'

'I shit on the Host man! If you build the bridge there no one will cross it in safety.'

'And how many bridges have you built?'

'Well, you can listen to me if you want, and I'm telling you . . .'

The polemic raged ever more ferociously and as one idea supplanted another, and the debate spun into a number of simultaneous arguments, the only thing everyone seemed to agree about was that Romero must have been either mad or drunk to choose such a ridiculous spot to build his bridge. The site was so utterly lacking in any of the desirable qualities, that the idea of simply rebuilding it didn't even merit consideration.

In the end, of course, we rebuilt it precisely where it was. Pedro had, perhaps, known something about his river.

First, with the help of twelve strong men all pulling and pushing in different directions we hauled the great eucalyptus trunks from the wood where Domingo and I had stacked them so many moons before. Then we rebuilt the first pier. We carried huge rocks over and dumped them in the edge of the river, everyone vying to heave the largest rock, reckless of almost certain hernias. Then we cut oleander and broom and branches of eucalyptus and made a thick bed of brush on top of the stones. Then another heavy bed of stones, then more brush and so on until we had a new pier jutting out over the river about five feet above the water-level.

The beams cost us a lot of effort to haul into place. We managed to heave the first one so that it jutted from the pier about two thirds of the way across the river. Everybody sat on it while Domingo, who had inevitably taken over the running of the operation, wobbled out along it with a rope. He leaped for the far bank and fell in the river.

'The Host! It's freezing!'

This was the signal for all the more impetuous men to try their luck. They all fell in the water but kept on going until it was decided that there were not enough men left to sit on the beam for support. Then we heaved it into its final position. It was too short. It lay with its far end well short of the bank.

No matter. Everybody slithered across it and set to rebuilding a great jutting pier on the far bank. Finally, after about four hours of work, we had two stout beams laid firmly from one rock-built pier to the other. We all sat on the bank, admiring the grace and elegance of our handiwork. It looked good and it cost nothing, but it was still almost impossible to cross in safety. I spent the next day gathering driftwood and nailing it across the beams to provide a flattish walkway. Domingo disapproved of the nails because they cost money.

'You don't spend money on the river. What's in the river is the river's. Sooner or later it will just rise up and sweep the lot off down to the sea.' I should have lashed the driftwood to the beams with ropes of woven esparto grass. That would have satisfied him.

The design of our new footbridge might have been basic but it had an intrinsic beauty and the driftwood walkway gave it a rather picturesque Himalayan look; simply to look at it made you want to cross it.

Sheep, however, have different sensibilities and, after discussing the matter with Domingo, I decided that it would be better to postpone introducing the new flock to El Valero and let them settle in first in a stable prepared on the town side of the river, beside La Colmena.

∾

No groom preparing a nuptial chamber for the arrival of his bride could have taken more care than I did in fixing the temporary stable. I mucked it out, scrubbed and disinfected it, and spent good money installing an automatic water-trough, a contrivance never before seen in the Alpujarra. As a finishing touch I roped up an old iron bedstead across the door and then waited, admiring my handiwork. The sheep arrived, and one by one I carried them down from the lorry, across the threshold. They huddled in a corner in the shadows.

Every day I walked across the river to feed the sheep their barley-straw and grains and to get them used to my presence. When I arrived, they would be lying trim, white and woolly, basking in the winter sunlight where it shone in shafts through the door and windows of the stable. As I entered, they would bound away in a panic and huddle in the far corner. Some days I would sit in the sunshine by the door and read or write letters. As they grew used to the idea of my being there, they gradually resumed their places and lay heaving gently, eyeing me with suspicion. If I moved a limb to scratch or turn a page they would stampede for the corner again and huddle in a mass of panting wool with seventy-four eyes and one resentful look directed at me. 153

Progress was slow. The sheep didn't seem to be getting used to me at all and I wondered how or if I could control the flock when I finally let them out of the stable and into the countryside. I had no dog. A normal established flock would have its *mansa* – its tame sheep – who would stick to the heels of the shepherd, and lead the rest of the flock. These lambs, having come from various different flocks, and being mostly young and therefore having no flocking instinct, would flee to the edges of the valley as soon as I opened the door.

After an abortive episode, best forgotten, with a couple of goats, Domingo suggested I marry the sheep up with his flock. We stuffed Domingo's dozen or so older ewes into the stable and fed them all together. It worked a treat; the next day, when we let them all out to graze on the hill above La Colmena, they stayed calmly together. Every day we took one or two of Domingo's sheep out, until we were left with just one.

'You can have that scraggy old thing,' said Old Man Domingo, to whom it belonged. 'It's never had a lamb but once and that was years ago. That sheep is good for nothing, but it'll be fine for your flock leader.'

The sheep in question was a bony old creature, with lop-ears, a permanent string of snot, and a craven look. She was also extremely wily. By a combination of cunning and thinness she managed time and again to insinuate herself into the special creep reserved for the ewe-lambs and wolf their extra rations. The creep was a fenced-off part of the stable with a tiny gap that only the lambs could get through. In the end we tied a stick to a piece of string around her neck, which would jam in the hole.

Thus our flock leader came to be known as Stick. She wore her impediment proudly like a badge of office as she tripped sniffling along at the head of the little flock, slavishly following the shepherd.

154

~

At the end of the sheep's first month, I took them up the hill to graze on the damp rosemary and thyme while I stood watching them through the wet mist, leaning on a crook. Below me wisps of cloud ebbed and flowed around the valley. As the sheep trod on the plants they released clouds of scent. From around the next ridge I could hear the bells of Domingo's tiny flock mingling with the rushing of the rivers.

Domingo appeared from below, dressed in his usual floppy blue cotton trousers and jacket and decomposing sneakers. We sat together on a wet rock.

'I can more or less manage the flock now with the help of Stick,' I told him. A heavy sneeze and a flying gobbet of mucus reminded me of the presence of that august animal. 'I might try and take them across to El Valero later on if I can persuade them to cross the bridge.'

'They'll be fine,' Domingo pronounced. 'Mine cross it now with no trouble at all.' We looked down on the bridge far below us, tiny and insubstantial in the distance.

That evening I took Stick at the head of the flock down to the river. Domingo followed behind. We all walked straight across the bridge except for one lamb – and there always is one – which decided not to chance the bridge but instead hurled itself into the racing river. I fished it out about fifty metres downstream, bedraggled and knocked about a bit by the rocks but otherwise unhurt. Waving good-bye to Domingo we set out slowly across the valley towards the stable at El Valero.

155

The morning after our successful crossing, I got up early, shaved, put on a clean T-shirt and went to let the sheep out to graze for the first time on El Valero soil, a lovingly prepared sward of grass in the river-fields.

There I sat on a bank by the stream, gazing at them as they stood up to their knees in grass and wild flowers beneath the orange trees. Sadly, the sheep didn't like it one bit. They stood there looking at me, wondering what to do. The poor creatures were right out of their element. As lambs they had spent their whole lives shut in stables eating straw and grains, and their mothers were mountain sheep, used to scuffling about on the hills in search of dry mouthfuls of woody aromatic plants.

Worried that I had made a serious miscalculation, I led them out of the fields and up into the dusty *secano*. They bounded happily into the scrub, and busied themselves nibbling at the sweet-scented herbs while I watched disconsolately, wondering what on earth I'd do with the lush grazing that I had so painstakingly nurtured.

Little by little, though, the sheep adapted themselves to my whims and came to start each day with a session on the grass. After a few days I no longer even had to walk them there. I would just open the stable gate in the morning and shut them in at night. They would spend the day ranging between the grass and the *secano* as the mood took them, and the farm rang to the sound of their bells during all the daylight hours.

Only Stick, having been used to following a shepherd all her life, seemed out of sorts. For months she would attach herself to anybody who happened to be passing through the farm, much to the discomfiture of occasional hikers making their way down from the hills.

BREEDING

OUR FIRST LAMBS WERE BORN IN APRIL. ON A BRIGHT SPRING morning I pushed open the stable door and discovered a steaming bundle of wet wool lying in the straw. A ewe was licking it happily and making the snickering noises that show maternal devotion in the ovine world. It was a small moment of triumph. Over the next two weeks El Valero shrank to the confines of the stable as Ana and I hung about the ewes ready to help them through any obstetric difficulty. Few showed an interest in the service. Unlike their overdomesticated British counterparts, the Segureñas have an independent nature. They seemed happy to wait for the stable door to creak shut again before depositing their slithery offspring, quietly and without much fuss, into nests that they had scrabbled in the straw.

Inevitably, one or two did need a bit of help and Ana was ready to oblige. Ana is good at lambing, her hands are smaller than mine and better suited to the agonisingly constricted manipulations between the ewe's pelvic bones to get the head or feet into the correct position for the exit. I was pleased to see her getting so involved after all her reservations about my sheep venture, although she was still far from enthusiastic about my plans for the expansion of the flock.

We kept the ewes and lambs penned close together for the first few days so the lambs could gather strength and bond strongly with their mothers; then we let them out.

'You shouldn't let the lambs out,' said Domingo.

'Why ever not?'

'The sun will eat them, and their lungs will fill with dust. Dealers round here don't like to buy lambs with the dirt of the *campo* on them.'

'What should we be doing, then?'

'You should separate them from the ewes when you let the sheep out in the morning, and leave the lambs in the stable.'

I looked at other shepherds' arrangements for this. Their lambs had a pretty dismal existence, shut in all day long in a stable where no ray of sunshine entered, though the little creatures were indomitable. Not even the most cramped and mephitic hell-hole can kill the joy of young animals. The slightest irregularity in the dung-packed floor became a hillock from which they would leap and, however tightly packed together, they lost no opportunity for racing round and high-tailing their legs in the air.

158

It was undeniable that the sun wouldn't eat the lambs in the stables, nor would their lungs clog with dust, and they certainly wouldn't lose weight through excessive exercise. They could address themselves precociously and earnestly to the business of eating high-protein concentrates and getting to killing weight as fast as possible.

Ana and I walked down to the river-fields to see how they were getting on. The newborn lambs were wandering about, gingerly sniffing the grass, startled by the terrors of snails, grasshoppers and butterflies. The older lambs, still snowy white and tiny, had gathered in a group and were busy hurtling in a mass along the raised bank of the *acequia* only to stop all of a sudden, turn back and race to their mothers, grab a quick drink of milk and fall asleep in the sunshine.

It was a sight to move even the stoniest-hearted profiteer and we decided to keep the lambs out. They have a short enough life anyway and I couldn't deny them some joy of it, not even in the interest of efficient husbandry.

A few weeks later I came home to find Domingo sitting on our terrace waiting to introduce me to his 'friend' Antonio Moya. As I climbed up the steps, sweating and dishevelled, the way I look after the lightest task, the creature seated beside Domingo uncoiled and advanced towards me, hand outstretched. It was enchanted to meet me; it had heard much about my exalted reputation and in the flesh I made such reports seem as shadows.

I stared open-mouthed at my flatterer, smooth-chested and meticulously groomed in his crisp white shirt, and gleaming with gold. Domingo's friend was the dealer El Moreno: the dark one. I found it difficult to believe that a man with such a face could possibly deal on business terms with the general public. His smile could have been applied with the briefest burst of an aerosol, his eyes lacked the warmth of a cobra's, and every line of his features, the dimple on his brow, the creases beside his mouth, the very set of his ears, spelt deceit.

159

'Such a beautiful farm . . . and what a lovely house. You must be very happy here.' He addressed me as one would a bat, staring at the shit-encrusted cave where it lived.

'It suits us.'

'I should think it does! You foreigners are so much cleverer than we Spanish.'

'And why would that be?'

'You choose such wonderful places to live. Domingo says you have some fine lambs to sell.' His smile narrowed.

'They're not bad, but they're not ready to sell yet.'

'I have seen them and I will give you a very fair price for them.'

'And how much would that be?'

'Five thousand apiece for the lot.'

'They're not ready yet.'

'I'll take them as they are.'

'Not for five thousand you won't.'

'But they're *camperos*, they've got the dust of the field on them.'

'I don't care, I'm not selling them till they're finished and it won't be at a price like that.'

There followed a rapidly delivered tirade of blandishments, against which I stood my ground admirably.

'Well, Cristóbal, it has been a pleasure – no, an honour – to do business with you. Until we meet again.' And El Moreno strode off with Domingo, cursing insistently in his ear as far as I could make out.

≈

'So that was your friend El Moreno?' I said next day to Domingo, a little puzzled by the apparent alliance.

'Yes, we used to work together. He lost his driving licence, so I used to drive him round, visiting shepherds, and he taught me all the tricks of the trade.'

'It must help a lot, knowing a dealer you can trust.'

'Trust? You must be joking! Sooner trust the serpent himself.'

'But you told me he was a friend . . .'

'Well, yes, he is, but he'd still screw me, just like anybody else. He screws everybody.'

'But what sort of friendship is that, for heaven's sake?'

160

'He does it for my own good, he says. It keeps me on my toes and teaches me a useful lesson. That way I avoid the pitfalls of being screwed by other dealers.'

'It seems to me an awful way to carry on. Are all dealers such shameless shits?'

'It's their job; it's the way the system works. They make their living by smooth talking, guile, knowing how to spin a story. It's a skill, just like whatever skill it is that you have that enables you to make a living from whatever it is that you do.'

Domingo has always been a little unsure as to how we make ends meet, as indeed am I.

'And by the same token it's a part of the shepherd's skill to cope with sharp dealers like El Moreno. A shepherd can't survive if he only knows how to walk with his sheep. He must also know how to sell them. It's the way life is, pitting one's wits against others. Take my cousin Manuel, for instance. Manuel is a hopeless case. He sold all his lambs to El Moreno the other day for four thousand. That's Manuel stuffed for the year now, penniless!'

'And you stood and watched?'

'Of course. I drove Moreno there.'

'And you didn't raise a finger to stop Manuel being screwed?'

'It's nature, isn't it? There's no point in saving a beetle from a blackbird . . . '

'But if the beetle happens to be your cousin . . . ?'

'Bah! you have to learn from the blackbird.'

El Moreno must have heard on the bush telegraph that the lambs were still for sale. The next time I saw him he turned up alone, considering himself now on terms of sufficient intimacy to dispense with the guidance of Domingo. It was five in the afternoon and we were sitting on the *tinao* with a couple of English friends who had driven over from Órgiva.

El Moreno clapped me on the back and told me of how he was barely able to contain his delight at seeing me again, made himself known and agreeable to the rest of the company, and sat down to drink wine while we all took tea. Our friends were enchanted by him. Within ten minutes the assembled company were hanging on his every word and vying for his attention.

It was then that he introduced the subject of the lambs. 'Let's go down and have a look at them and see how they've got on,' he suggested.

We leaned on the stable gate and gazed into the crowded pen.

I waited for Moreno to get the deal rolling . . . nothing. He considered the lambs in glum silence. I was the first to break.

'Well?'

'Well, they haven't grown much, have they?'

'They'll be a good twenty kilos.'

'Never!'

'They weigh heavy, these Segureñas. All meat, you know.'

'So, how much do you want for them?'

'They are a good weight, and unless I'm mistaken the price has gone up . . . so if you take them all you can have them for six thousand pesetas each . . . '

'No good, the price is much lower than that.'

'. . . but if you want to select the best, then seven thousand.'

El Moreno shook his head and slipped into gear. 'Hold this.' He proferred a heavy bundle of notes. 'I'm offering you four thousand five hundred – that's nine hundred duros – and how many did you say there were? Thirty-seven lambs? That makes thirty-three thousand, three hundred duros – here it is in notes. Go on, count it . . . '

Now I consider myself fast enough with mental arithmetic for a negotiation on the price of some sheep, but I clearly wasn't in the same league as El Moreno. His speed and accuracy were astonishing. He knew he had the advantage over me in this, but he was deliberately adding to my confusion by calculating partly in pesetas and partly in duros.

A duro is five pesetas and a common unit of currency throughout Spain. Often older people cannot compute in simple pesetas; one day in the bakery I heard a customer saying, 'What do I owe you, Mari-Carmen?' 'Three hundred and ninety-five pesetas,' came the reply. 'Don't be silly woman. What's that in duros?' 'Seventy-nine.' 'Right then. Now we understand one another.'

As El Moreno spread the money, I kept my hands firmly behind my back and looked at the wall so as not to be hypnotised by that great wad of notes.

'Hold these!'

'Look, I'm not taking four thousand five hundred, nor five thousand. I said six.'

'Alright then, if you must' – and he grabbed my arm and slapped a tempting ten-thousand-peseta note into my quivering palm. Then he began counting again, interleaving crisp large notes with smaller grubbier ones of much lower denomination, and all the time switching between duros and pesetas in a low hypnotic numerical chant.

'Umm . . . I've lost count.'

'Right, let's start again, ten, twenty, thirty,' and off he went, slapping note after note on the pile.

163

The lambs considered us with suspicion from their huddle in the corner of the pen. Moreno had me right where he wanted. Apart from the dazzling arithmetical gymnastics his trick seemed to have something to do with making sure that I was always holding some of his money, and never giving a straight answer to my questions.

'I've lost it,' I pleaded. 'How much are you offering me now anyway?'

'I'm giving you a hell of a good deal here, you won't get nine hundred and eighty duros anywhere else and that's my top price.'

'Well, I'm not selling them below five thousand five hundred. You know as well as I do that they're a gift at that.'

'Look, you've dragged me all the way out here . . .'

'You invited yourself.'

'I've come all this way and wasted a lot of time. I'm a busy man and I haven't time for this sort of foolery.' Saying which he strode off angrily down the hill. I started up towards the house.

'Dammit,' I muttered to myself. I couldn't afford to lose the sale. 'Perhaps I asked too much . . .' I turned to find Moreno at my elbow.

'Here, hold your hand out – count this – five, seven . . .'

I sold them in the end for five thousand two hundred apiece: that is to say one thousand and forty duros. The price for the lot was one hundred and ninety-two thousand four hundred pesetas – or thirty-eight thousand four hundred and eighty duros. Thank heavens Spanish sheep dealers don't have guineas, pounds, shillings and pence in their armoury.

The buyer pays about ten percent as a deposit and then pays the rest when he comes to fetch the lambs. The next day El Moreno turned up with a lorry and four confederates. We counted the lambs from the stable into the lorry. Now you wouldn't have thought that a dispute could arise over the matter of counting thirty-seven lambs one by one. But it did. So skilled were these men in the art of deceit that I seriously doubted my own ability to count.

164

~

Five thousand two hundred pesetas was far from being a good price for the lambs, and it might seem odd that I eventually decided to do business with a man whom I so utterly mistrusted.

I had a good reason, though. We had had no better offer and we needed the money. Not long after El Moreno's first visit, Ana had made an announcement that forcibly brought home to us the value of ready cash.

'I think I'm pregnant, Chris,' she said. It was an otherwise perfectly normal day. We were standing on the *tinao* sorting out a sack of almonds and watching the sheep munching their way through the wilderness.

'Pregnant,' I repeated absently.

'I'm going to have a baby.'

'You're having a baby . . . but . . . but . . ?'

I shuffled my feet before her, not quite sure how to arrange my limbs and features. There was too long a moment of confusion before I managed the right sort of grin and hugged her with exaggerated care.

'God, that's wonderful . . . I . . . er . . . hell, I hardly know what to say . . .' We laughed nervously. This is said to be one of the key moments in life, and there I was messing it up.

It wasn't that I didn't want a baby. I did. Children had for a long time been part of the grand plan in moving to El Valero, but despite our best efforts they hadn't turned up and in the meantime other plans and pleasures had come creeping into the space I had reserved for fatherhood. I wondered, too, if we were really the right sort of people to take on this awesome responsibility. Was the eccentric lifestyle we had chosen the right thing for a creature as delicate as a baby? Running beneath all this disquiet was a deep vein of delight that I was scrabbling to reach.

That evening we opened a better bottle of wine than we might otherwise have drunk and illuminated our omelette and tomato salad with a candle and some flowers. Our supper conversation ranged over the new rogue element that we would now have to take into our calculations, but our words were carefully chosen so as not to tempt fate by anything too emphatic. If we hadn't known ourselves to be sublimely content we might have each thought the other just a little depressed.

A few days later I telephoned my mother to tell her the news. This would be her first grandchild.

'It appears, Mum, that at long last you're going to be a grand-mother.'

She was silent for an instant, and then she seemed to burst with happiness. I had never experienced anybody 'bursting with happiness' before and even filtered through international telephone cables, or zinging through the ionosphere, it blew me away. 'Well,' I thought, 'who knows what this baby will be like, or what my part in its existence will do to me? But just to hear that happiness in my mother's voice makes it all worthwhile.'

I told Domingo, too, apropos of nothing. '*En hora buena* – congratulations,' he replied, then added in an unusually thoughtful tone, 'I've told you before that a baby is what you need at El Valero. You'll get lonely all by yourselves on the wrong side of the river.' And he returned to swatting a horsefly that was gorging itself on the blood of Bottom's belly.

~

At the beginning of October I went to Sweden to spend a month shearing sheep. It may seem odd to go sheep-shearing in a Nordic country just as the winter comes on, but this was the way the Swedes liked it. I would go in October when the sheep were about to be housed for the winter, and then again in March just before they lambed. Swedish sheep, or most of them at any rate, need shearing twice a year, which was fine for me from a financial point of view, but a source of grief to the Swedish sheep-farmers, who had to pay for two shearings and earned nothing at all for the wool.

I had been going to Sweden twice a year for fifteen years but somehow, despite having some good friends there, that Nordic utopia had failed altogether to find a place in my heart. I found myself swamped by the lugubrium of the uncontaminated but dreary landscape and bored by the dullness of its spiritless towns and cities. I would drive sometimes for days through interminable pine forests in the snow to get to far-off farms where I would shear flocks of black sheep in dark barns beneath the dismal light of the glowering northern sky. The money was spectacularly good (and we would be needing it with a baby to take care of) but it was hard to stay cheerful.

During my previous trips Ana had looked after the farm on her own – '*Ay, que valiente!*' local people would say when they heard. 'To stay all on your own in a terrible place like that, *ay por dios!*' But this time a friend of our Dutch neighbours, Belinda, a woman we had come to know well, offered to stay with Ana and keep her company. Belinda was a handy sort of a woman who amongst other things knew a thing or two about midwifery.

The shearing usually took about a month, and Ana had calculated that the baby would arrive round about the middle of November. Without the presence of Belinda I think we both would have felt a little uneasy.

~

Sweden passed even slower than usual that month, but at last I had completed the business and, with a boosted bank balance and a bag stuffed with pickled fish, smoked salmon and Swedish cheese-slicers, found myself back on the bus to Órgiva. It hauled its way up the long winding inclines from the coast into the mountains south of Granada just as the last rays of evening sunshine were setting on the snow-clad peaks. What a wonderful place to be born, I thought.

It was dark by the time I arrived at the bus station but Ana was there to meet me. She had been showing clear signs of the presence of somebody else inside her when I left and now there was no mistaking her condition. She moved self-consciously, with a slight backward lean to counterweight the swelling dome of her belly. We embraced tentatively and I stood back to admire the extraordinary phenomenon of two-persons-in-one.

'I'm certainly glad to have you back, I don't think it's going to be long now,' she said as I started up the Landrover.

'I'm glad, too, I can tell you. God, it's good to be home.'

The occasional absence is a great tonic for any relationship. I was always pleased to see Ana, but after a month in Sweden thinking shadowy thoughts of antenatal emergencies – well, I was ecstatic. She looked good and healthy, too, blooming as the cliché goes, and surprisingly at ease with the drama ahead.

∼

Back at the farm, the sheep also looked fat and happy, and the dark green globes of the oranges on the trees were full of the promise of sweet fruit about to ripen. The ground beneath the odd fig tree that the sheep couldn't get to was spattered with rotten purple fruit.

It took Ana to point out to me that there was also a rather bare look to the place. She really seemed quite concerned. In my absence, the sheep had been getting out of control, working their way through the farm, clearing the undergrowth and mowing the grass down to the level of the dust. That in itself was no cause for alarm but Ana pointed out places where the stone walls of the terracing had begun to crumble and fall, leaving dusty paths and hillocks of earth and stones.

Sheep tend not to go round the end of a wall to get on or off a terrace – they all jump up or down together in the middle – and a hundred and more little hooves at a time had started to take their toll. They had also climbed onto the wire protectors I had put round the new apricot trees, and nibbled the tops off. They had invaded the garden and eaten the buddleia and all the palm trees we'd put in; and then finally they had burst into and laid waste the holy of holies, Ana's vegetable patch. They didn't think much of the aubergines and chillis but had wolfed the rest.

'I fear they're going to turn the place into a desert,' said Ana gloomily.

'Maybe that would be better than the jungle it would be without them.'

'I think I prefer the jungle with its flowers and greenery.'

'Yes, you're right . . . but I'm sure we'll find a way of dealing with them,' I said, stretching lazily out on my favourite corner of the terrace. 'You can't get everything right first try, can you?'

~

I'm not quite sure how I expected to spend those last fleeting moments of freedom before parenthood began; sitting, perhaps, on the terrace with Ana, sipping tea and indulging in whatever reveries the landscape triggered. I hadn't imagined that I would be cast out each morning to wander the farm clutching a bucket of watered-down dog-turd.

Canina, as this concoction is known, was recommended to Ana as an excellent sheep deterrent and she was determined that I should liberally spatter each of our trees with it. Now, I was as concerned as Ana about the future of our orange and olive trees, and I knew better than to interfere with the nesting instincts of a very pregnant woman, but it was beyond me to accept this task with good grace.

Skill is paramount in the dousing and flicking of the esparto grass brush and there are obvious and unsavoury consequences to getting it wrong. I suffered all of them. There was also the dis-

169

heartening knowledge that the deterrent effect would wear off, especially after a heavy rain, and that the moment you finish coating the last tree the sheep will be beginning some tentative nibbles at the first.

My afternoons were equally hectic. These were spent erecting some rudimentary fences to guide the sheep away from the vulnerable areas on the farm, beginning with the stalag perimeter fence that Ana had designed for her vegetable patch. If Ana had ever had a soft spot for sheep, those days were past. A stoical tolerance was the best they could hope for now.

CHLOË AND THE IMMACULATE CONCEPTION

'LOOK, I'M SORRY, BUT YOU'LL HAVE TO LEAVE THE ROOM. IF you faint again and fall and crack your head on the tiles, there's nothing we can do for you. We've got too much going on to worry about you.'

So I left and gazed morosely out of the corridor window at the earth-moving machines pecking away like huge birds at the footings of Granada's new ring road, and tried to blot out for a moment the image of Ana sweating and heaving in the hospital delivery theatre. And what was it all for? So that the lives we had both been rather enjoying could change in some irrevocable way, perhaps for the worse? Had there been a beer-can handy I would have kicked out at it malevolently. But the immaculate corridors of the Hospital of the Immaculate Conception offered no such solace.

The drama had begun the night before. Ana had shaken me awake at two in the morning complaining that her waters had burst. I was to bring her some tea and digestive biscuits and then get the car ready while she cleaned the bathroom. Obviously, I had misheard about the bathroom. Weren't we supposed to drive like the wind to the city, screeching to a halt in the hospital fore-court? Apparently not. It was half past two on that mild November night before Ana handed me a wet floorcloth and bucket and at last let me help her into the Landrover.

A full moon was hanging above the dark citrus leaves as we bumped and rattled our way out of the valley towards sleeping Granada. At the bend by the road to the dump in Lanjarón we were brought to a halt – some men were blasting the hill away in the interest of road safety. We had to turn round and drive back through Órgiva, out across the Seven-Eye bridge, and make a long detour to Granada via the coast.

The still night air, scented with pine, had a dream-like quality, and the impression was heightened by soft shadows and silver light. Neither of us have forgotten the beauty of that journey. We stopped so that Ana could have a pee and look at the moon for a bit before we joined the main road for the long haul up the mountains to Granada. She was having contractions every five minutes or so by then, but kept assuring me that they were mild and not really too painful.

As we entered the city the first grey light of dawn spread down from the mountains to join the streetlights. I pulled straight into the hospital emergency bay.

'You can't park here,' said Ana. 'This is for emergencies.'

'But we are an emergency, surely?'

'Do as I say. Park the car in the ordinary people's car park over there.'

'Very well, dear.' It seemed unwise to argue with Ana when she was having contractions.

We walked unhurriedly through the doors of the emergency department. I felt small and unimportant as they took Ana's details. Modern man is supposed to be present at the birth of his babies, and I, true to form, was keen to be there and hold Ana's hand should she require such a service. But this innovation had not yet arrived in provincial Spain, so in order to get in I had to stoop to trickery.

'I must be with my wife because she doesn't speak Spanish and I may have to translate for her,' I lied. Ana had just given her details in perfectly fluent Castellano.

'It is not normal, but if you must.'

'I must,' I insisted, and then Ana was whisked away.

Soon I was ushered into a brightly lit theatre, where I found Ana, clad in a white smock and lying with her legs dangling from stirrups, on top of a strange, green contraption. The arrangement put me in mind of a modern ducking stool. Beside her a bank of electronic boxes hummed and beeped and glittered with lights.

I hadn't given much thought to the subject of birthing rooms until then. One of the travellers in the valley had regaled us with the details of a birth in a candle-lit teepee, where bongo-drummers and untrained flautists had provided ambient music, while seventeen women linked hands around the labouring woman and circled her, chanting. Such descriptions, coupled with our fears of being cut off by the river, did a lot to reinforce our choice of an early admission to a hospital in Granada. As I looked around, however, I felt rather wistful about the teepee. 173

Ana smiled nervously at me through a tangle of wires and held out her hand. Two stocky young men in leather bomber-jackets entered.

'Hola,' they grinned. 'We're the midwives.'

They washed and changed in a businesslike manner and

connected Ana to what they said was a digital contraction-measuring device. Each time she had a contraction, which was every couple of minutes now, red lights flashed on the machine and a reading of the intensity of the contraction appeared on the screen. '2' it said quietly, then '2' again . . . and again '2'. Ana was contracting comfortably. Somebody inside her was languorously considering making an entrance.

But these '2's were not good enough for the midwives, so they plumbed Ana into some sort of a drip. '16' screamed the machine, as in an instant the gentle contractions became body-bursting convulsions. '16' . . . '19' – oh Lord, I thought she was going to burst. It was hot and airless in that awful place. My legs buckled slowly beneath me.

I'll spare you the details. Ana's last stage of labour ran for an hour and a half, which I'm told is not much, but seemed to me an eternity of pain. Ana sweated and pushed and said she thought her eyes were going to burst. I squeezed her hand and fainted yet again. So they sent me out to stand in the corridor.

It really did seem awful. Those moments that should have been full of joy and wonder – the arrival of a new person on earth – were clouded over by images of Ana convulsed with pain. When I returned from my exile in the corridor, I could see that the midwives were getting worried; they kept trying to contact the head of the gynaecology department for help but the man was nowhere to be found. The contraction machine flashed astronomical numbers. A device hooked up to the baby, measuring heartbeats, pulses, whatever, registered lower and lower. Its warning lights started flashing. Electronic alarms went off. 'Don't faint – don't faint,' I muttered to myself, keeping hold of Ana's hand. They were all too busy to notice when I picked myself up yet again from the floor.

And then a great heave and at last it was out. Ana sagged, limp

and exhausted but still alive. A blue rubbery thing was plonked
on a towel on the sideboard.

'*Es normal?*' I asked. I couldn't bring myself to look at the blue
thing yet; I was interested only in Ana.

'*Si, es normal.*'

∾

I slipped out to buy flowers and wine – anything to restore some
cheer after the ordeal in that dreadful chamber. When I returned
Ana was lying in stiff white sheets. She smiled feebly. Beside her
bed was a cot with the sheet drawn fully up over its small occupant's head. I gave her the flowers and kissed her more tenderly
than I had done in a long time. I thought I'd almost lost her.

'You'd better have a look at the baby,' she said after a while.

Without much enthusiasm I rose and pulled back the sheet.
There was that hideous purple head with thin strands of wet hair
clagged to the top. I looked down at the sleeping baby. Surely you
couldn't love such a thing . . . or could you? Something was happening . . . it was as if a wave of warm emotion washed over me.
I trembled as I gazed at the little creature. I was transfixed,
enslaved. All the hormones and juices that had so far failed to
turn up and do their stuff engulfed me in a tide of love. I
plumped back down on the bed, flaccid and speechless, and tried
to tell Ana what was happening. The words wouldn't come out.

'I know,' she smiled. 'It's just happened to me too.'

It was some hours before I could wrench myself away from the
side of the cot and drive back to feed the animals. I had momentous news to impart.

Chloë had arrived among us.

175

∾

A few days later we bundled Chloë up and drove her home. El Valero seemed a rough, brutish home for such a delicate little creature. The sunshine and the flowers, the lovely view of rivers and mountains and the profound peace of the place seemed too easily eclipsed by the scorpions and centipedes, the snakes and eagles, the smothery cats lying in her cradle, the huge dogs looking with predatory interest at the small baby.

Beaune, we knew, would be safe, but we were a little worried that Bonka would be jealous of the new arrival and perhaps vent her spleen by eating her. In the event there was nothing to fear. Bonka started by appearing to be completely unaware of Chloë's existence, and then, when this attitude became unsustainable, accepted her as a fully fledged member of the household. Chloë adored both the dogs and seemed to adopt Beaune as an extension of herself, rolling about with her and curling up to sleep in her basket, so that it was with difficulty that we managed to persuade her that she was really human. We scotched the cats' natural instinct to smother her by draping a fruit-net over the cradle. As for the attentions of the scorpions and centipedes and other undesirables, we just kept our fingers crossed.

Chloë seemed to thrive in her harsh environment. A constant stream of well-wishers, drawn by the magic of a new baby, braved the rigours of the river and the valley track to come and see her. One afternoon Domingo turned up with his parents bearing bags of sugar. Sugar is a traditional gift for newborn babies here in the Alpujarra. Expira was ecstatic about Chloë, showing her approval in the time-honoured way by pinching the poor little thing's cheeks and clucking over her.

'I told you that you must have babies,' she enthused, 'and now look what a precious little sweet thing you've gone and produced! You must have more, there's no time to lose.'

Domingo, who had at first confined himself to glancing occasionally at Chloë from behind his parent's back, stepped forward

176

and gathered her gently and skilfully in his arms. He did it like someone who has practised all his life, cradling her head as he rocked her. I wasn't that good at it myself yet, having only just had the technique demonstrated to me in the hospital, and looked on in wonder as Domingo strolled outside with her, carefully shielding her face from the harsh sunlight.

We saw quite a lot of Domingo during Chloë's first months and he would often sweep her up from her blanket and take her for a short walk on the hill by the house. She seemed as contented in his arms as in her own mother's. A part of me envied him this facility – I was fine with Chloë but no good at all with other people's babies. However, most of all I was saddened by Domingo's conviction that he would never become a father himself.

'It's impossible,' he would say tersely, putting an end to the subject. 'I barely make enough money to keep myself alive. How could I ever support a wife and children?'

There seemed a terrible earnestness in Domingo's words. He had clearly resigned himself to remaining a bachelor, rather than risk bringing up children in poverty, and it hurt me sorely to see it. You don't have to be a particularly good judge of character to recognise what a great father Domingo would make. But then Domingo had grown up in a different world from the one I had known. He had witnessed what hunger and deprivation could do to families.

177

~

As those first months passed and we all settled into our new existence together, I realised just what friends had meant when they tried to explain to me the joy of having one's own child. No matter how eloquently it had been described, nobody had been able to get anywhere near the real experience. We looked back on all our previous worries about how our lives would be changed and disrupted, and were shocked by how irrelevant those thoughts now seemed. It was as if we had just been handed the key to crack the next part of the code of existence. The various loves in me grew and grew, and all as a result of this new being who had come to stay in our home. And to think that we might have gone through life without ever having let this happen to us.

~

Chloë's first word was 'Beaune'. She pronounced it with such relish that her fool of a father was enchanted, despite having to wait some weeks to gain equal footing with the dog. Her first sentence, when it came, also concerned Beaune, but it was heartrending to hear.

Ana and Chloë had come to the bus-stop to meet me when I returned from another autumn sheep-shearing season in Sweden. 'Beaune,' Chloë squeaked as I lifted her up for a hug. 'Beaune gone.'

It was true. Beaune had succumbed to a form of distemper only a week after I had left, and had died within days. Ana was absolutely desolate and so was Chloë. Arriving at the farm we processed solemnly, Chloë pointing the way, to the patch on a neglected olive terrace where Ana had buried her dog.

In the consoling way that nature sometimes contrives, we dis-covered that week that Bonka was pregnant. She produced a lit-ter of eight puppies, of which we kept two; one because it had the same markings as its mother, the other because it had one ear sticking up and the other drooping down. They were known as Barkis and Bodger and became Chloë's constant companions as they grew up together.

178

As a farm-girl, birth and death came to be part of Chloë's everyday experience. She watched lambs being born before she was one year old, and seemed to take in her stride the dispersal of the rest of Bonka's puppies and the dispatching of the odd chicken or sheep.

As she approached two, one of her favourite treats was an expedition to the cave in the river to see the dead goat. An ailing goat from one of the flocks that grazed in the riverbed had crept into a cave to die where the rivers join. We came across the carcass, bloated and torn by wild animals, evil-smelling and moving with a living mat of flies. The eyes were long gone. The goat gazed across the reeds through bloody sockets.

'I must keep her from this ghastly sight,' I thought, trying to insinuate myself between Chloë and the cave.

'What's that?' she asked, jabbing an imperious finger towards the cave.

'What's what?'

'That, there.'

'Oh, that. It's just a dead goat.'

'Chloë see goat,' she insisted, dragging me by the arm towards the cave.

She was delighted by it. She had none of the revulsion that we adults feel for such things. Every day she would clamour to go and see the dead goat, as it slowly decomposed and disappeared, gnawed away by foxes and birds and dog. I too came to look forward to our expeditions, to see how the thing was progressing, the goat's very solid presence reverting gradually to nothing. Had we lived in the city we would perhaps have gone every day to the park. The advantages of country living are not all immediately obvious.

179

∼

'Who made us, Daddy?' Chloë sprung the question a few weeks after her second birthday.

'I'm not sure about that one, Chloë,' I countered. 'I think your mother knows, though.'

With skill and tact I deflect the more awkward questions to the higher authority. I like to think, though, that I make a slightly better showing on the simpler ones.

'Air isn't anything, is it?' Chloë asked one day.

I was rather pleased with that question from a two-year-old. I have read that when Aldous Huxley was six, he was seen to be lost in thought, and when asked what he was thinking about, he had replied 'skin'. To be thinking about air before reaching three was good, I thought. It showed an aptitude for reflection, a curiosity that would set her off on the right track for the various improbable futures I have planned for her. I would have to deal with this question seriously.

'Yes, it is something, as a matter of fact.'

'What then?'

'Well, it's lots of things, mostly gases ...'

'What's gases?'

'Well – er – gases are rather like air ... you can't see them ... or not usually, though I suppose some look like smoke. Gas comes in the orange bottles we use for the cooker ... er ...'

'Can you tie my Barbie's hair?'

'Alright.'

As I tied the wretched Barbie's ponytail, cackfingered, I thought about the inadequacy of my answer. What the hell was air anyway? How could I better explain gases? I'd made a muck of that one – probably arrested her development.

Chloë looked on thoughtfully as I fumbled with the detestable doll. 'Houses aren't anything, are they?'

I turned round and looked at our house. It wasn't much but it was certainly something, and I was rather proud of having built

180

it. I thought of the stones we had hauled up from the river, heaved onto the scaffolding, and – not unskilfully – eased into place. It's difficult to estimate the weight of a stone house, but surely it must be a hundred tons or more.

'Well, this house is something; it's stones and cement and sand and water and wood and canes and mud . . . and lots of work.'

She mused on this for a while.

'Which Barbie do you think is the more beauty, this one or the pink one?'

FRIENDS AND FOREIGNERS

HOWEVER MUCH YOU MAY FIGHT AGAINST IT, IF YOU LIVE abroad where there are other expatriates, you become part of what is known as the Foreign Community. Initially, I struggled hard against this notion but as the years passed I grew more relaxed about my status as a foreigner and more willing to appreciate the ties that, by language, humour and shared experience, bound me to my compatriots.

Being a part of a foreign community is a bit like being at school. Among other things seniority bestows respect. In our part of the Alpujarras, the most senior member by age, time served, and a natural proclivity towards seniority, was Janet. She had moved here in the early Seventies and built a large house on the outskirts of Tijolas, at the beginning of our valley, which she proceeded to enclose with a highly imposing wall.

Romero once told me with a smirk of how a horsedealer of his acquaintance had once scaled these walls. He tethered his horse nearby and swung himself up with the aid of a stout creeper and a handy tree. His intention, once inside the garden, was undoubtedly to surprise the lady occupant, but his plan went badly wrong. As he dropped from the wall into the shrubbery, he was set upon by Janet's pack of Appenzeller dogs, one of which gave him a nasty bite in the arse. He flew back over the wall and rode painfully into town where he promptly denounced Janet to the police for keeping a dangerous animal.

For those with less nefarious intentions there's a small blue door that you can knock upon. Ana and I, having been invited to lunch by Janet the summer after we moved to El Valero, knocked and waited politely, as befits newcomers visiting the gentry. The top half of the door flew open to reveal her pack of slavering dogs. Janet stood amongst them, knuckles clenched round the handle of a long leather whip which she flailed to left and right, cursing the dogs roundly.

'Come in, come in, quickly, quickly, and don't mind the dogs. Just keep your hands above your heads, they'll get used to you. Down, you bugger!' And with a deft boot and a lash of the whip she floored a particularly disagreeable specimen that was hovering around our throats.

We shuffled in, hands up, and the door slammed behind us. 'Welcome, my dears!' shouted Janet above the awful din. 'Wait there a minute while I deal with these brutes. Some meat should keep them quiet.' She disappeared with the dogs at her heels, leaving us trembling by the door. Soon she returned with half a dozen split cow's heads, red and meaty, which she hurled onto the lawn. The dogs crashed through the shrubbery and leapt in slobberous delight upon the head-bones.

'These are my children, you see,' beamed Janet as she discarded her whip. 'Now, what shall we drink before lunch?'

We settled for wine and sat down at the table beneath a vine-covered trellis – one of a sequence of DIY-looking follies. Lawns dotted with exotic trees rolled across to a huge stone-flagged

183

pool with a classical gazebo at the end. We sipped our wine and gasped politely at the garden.

'You must excuse me a minute, I'm just putting the finishing touches to the lunch. Help yourselves to more wine.'

We helped ourselves and went to admire a fish-pond, full of fish and frogs, among them a tiny green tree-frog that Janet had imported from exotic climes. Sitting down again I noticed a snake lying by the pond contentedly eating a fish.

'Now there's a most singular phenomenon,' I remarked to Ana.

'Perhaps we should say something . . . '

'Janet, is there supposed to be a snake eating fish by the pond?'

'What?' from the kitchen.

'A snake, there's a snake eating your fish.'

She shot out of the kitchen. 'A snake? Where? . . . so there is. I know him – he's been taking all the fish for the last couple of months. This time I'm going to fix the bastard. Wait, Chris, hold him there while I get something to kill him with. I know what'll settle his hash! Hang on there, don't whatever you do let him go!' and she shot back into the kitchen.

I looked quizzically at Ana, and back at the snake.

'How the hell am I supposed to keep it there?'

The snake fortunately didn't seem much disposed to move. It was still peacefully eating its fish . . . or rather Janet's fish. I could hear a frenzied rummaging in the kitchen, and furious cries.

'Where oh where is the bloody meat tenderiser? Where in the name of hell has the thing gone?! . . . there it is! Is he still there, Chris? You still got him?'

'Yes, still here.'

She came hurtling out of the kitchen, brandishing the meat-tenderiser, leapt into the bushes and lunged for the snake with her weapon, whereupon the head of the utensil fell off.

'Buggery! Now the head's come off! Can't they make decent

184

tools in this accursed country? And now the bloody snake's slithered off again.'

She sat down at the table and took a slug of wine.

'Oh well, it was a damn good try. Perhaps I'll get him next time. Right, let there be luncheon!'

And she produced a sumptuous six-course Indian meal, all freshly prepared. As we worked our way through it she told us the story of her life. How she was thwarted by the Mau Mau uprising in her attempts to qualify as a vet in Kenya, and forced instead to study the subject at home, coming through with a pretty thorough knowledge of animal ailments and their treatment. She now runs a free clinic from her home and does a first-rate job of fixing up all the local cats, dogs and horses. Doing this she enjoys her happiest hours.

When she is not attending to sick animals, Janet told us, she studies. She was currently working through maths and physics and veterinary science, and in order to prevent her outlook on life becoming too earnest, was reading Swiss satirical magazines in French and German. Try as I might, I found it impossible to imagine the Swiss as a fund of satirical humour. I said as much to Janet. 'Yes . . . yes, Chris, you're perfectly right. They don't have any humour at all. In fact, the Swiss have the sort of sense of humour you'd expect a dog to have!'

Thank heavens for Janet, she's a true eccentric and, for all her bluffness, unfailingly generous. She has also become a staunch friend of Chloë's. 'I've never had much time for babies, Ana,' she boomed on her first visit after Chloë's birth. 'Animals are a lot less trouble and serve you better too as a general rule. But I have to say that's a damn fine baby you've got there. I'll tell you what I'm going to do, I'm going to knit it a parrot. Nice little fellow like that, what it needs is a proper woollen parrot. I used to be pretty good at knitting years ago, you know, but it got in the way of the veterinary studies, so I stopped it.'

185

Sure enough, within a couple of weeks a bright woollen parrot, an amorphous woollen bag with a couple of flaps on the side and two buttons for the eyes, turned up. Janet had also knitted a white tam-o-shanter – to keep the little fellow's head warm. Stuffed with straw it would have made a handy pack-saddle for a donkey. But that was not all: she had also carpentered a beautiful high-chair with the seat upholstered apparently in some rare tribal cloth, and made a wooden chest to keep Chloë's clothes in. Treasured gifts.

∿

There seems to be a preponderance of eccentric women among the foreigners here. Some of them have husbands in tow, but they tend to be vapid creatures who fade into the background and are of little account. Amanda and Malcolm are one such couple: typical, in their way, of the Órgiva New Agers. Malcolm has long white hair and a penchant for loose flowing clothes. Rodrigo, whose flock of goats ravages the wilderness around Amanda and Malcolm's land, is unable to accept that Malcolm is a man. Rodrigo always refers to them, and he refers to them a lot, as there are constant disputes between them, as 'those two Englishwomen'.

Before coming to Spain, Amanda made a living as an organic farmer on the Welsh borders, and in the Alpujarras she was soon recognised among the ex-pat community as the person to consult on all matters horticultural and botanical. I sought her out one hot June morning to ask her advice about *Lavatera olbia*, a flowering shrub that is indigenous to central and western Andalucía. A friend in England, who is a seed-merchant, had started giving us the odd order for wild flower seeds, and had asked for a kilo of the *lavatera*. Try as I might, I couldn't find a single specimen of the plant. So I set out with Chloë gurgling

186

away on the seat beside me, on an expedition to try Amanda's botanical expertise.

I came upon her, clad in white muslin, thumping away with a mattock in her vegetable patch. As I bounced along the rough mountain track that led to her home, she straightened up as she saw me, swept the hair from her eyes and asked: 'Who is this that comes to visit me when the moon is rising in Aquarius?'

People had told me about Amanda's enthusiasm for astrology but even so the question caught me off my guard. I looked down to see if Chloë could shed any light on the issue, but she had succumbed to the noonday heat and fallen fast asleep.

'Er . . . my name's Chris, Chris Stewart. I'm told you're an expert botanist. I need some information about some plants that might grow around here.'

'People are very kind to say that. I'm sure it's not true, but let's have some tea anyway and I'll see if I can help you out.'

Amanda had not come across any of the *lavatera* I was after but was clearly a repository of knowledge on Alpujarran flora. We drank tea beneath a rose-covered arbour and talked about botany, the mountains and Rodrigo, as we gazed across the Mediterranean at the faint outline of the Rif in Morocco. Chloë, meanwhile, dozed on in my lap.

'Rodrigo is too bad, you know, his goats are absolutely destroying the countryside. I've told him about it time and again but he takes not a blind bit of notice. Soon Rodrigo and his wretched goats will have us living in a desert. You do know, don't you, that the Sahara Desert was a green and fertile garden until Rodrigo and his ilk started having their way with it?'

'I had heard of such a thing, yes.'

'Well, the answer, I'm convinced, is to plant retama all over the dry parts of the mountains. Retama will put up with pretty much anything . . . except goats.'

'Retama? You can't be serious!'

187

Retama is a tall woody shrub with long silver leaves and deep roots. In spring it scents the hills and valleys throughout southern Spain with its pendulous showers of yellow blooms. There's an awful lot of it about and it's of little apparent use. Persuading Rodrigo to plant retama on the hills would be like trying to get a British dairy-farmer to sow docks and thistles.

'I'm perfectly serious,' she insisted. 'Retama is the thing. I have actually had a talk with Rodrigo about my idea, and I do believe he is slowly coming round to it.'

'I'm the first one to approve of a bit of original thinking,' I said, trying not to be dismissive, 'but I can't really see the idea taking root, so to speak. Retama is pretty, and it's drought-resistant with those long long roots, but beyond providing a bit of seed and frond for the goats to . . .'

'Wretched goats! I'm not going to plant it for the goats, Chris. In order to build up a viable ecology in this area we must start to get the goats out of the equation.'

We talked around the subject until it was exhausted, Chloë was awake, and her supper beckoned. I made my excuses, casting a lunch invitation for Sunday as I started the Landrover. 'Oh – and bring your . . . bring, er . . .'

'Malcolm, you mean Malcolm, I take it. Yes, I'll bring him, too.'

~

'That,' said Amanda, pushing back the sleeves of her muslin dress and jabbing at the fly-trap that I'd hung on the stable wall, 'that is a disgusting contraption. How could you do that?'

The offending trap was an American patent and a device of which I was rather proud. It consisted of a plastic bag full of water and some mephitic muck that is apparently so irresistible to flies that they crawl happily through a plastic funnel in order to drown themselves alongside a sodden and evil-smelling mass of their peers. I was lured into buying it by the bizarre testimonial emblazoned across the packet: 'With your wonderful flytrap we were able to enjoy our annual barbecue without flies. Where we have our barbecue is right by the hogpens!'

'Surely, Amanda, one has to draw the line somewhere,' I protested, 'and flies fall a long way beneath the line I've drawn. Look at the misery they cause the horses and sheep, to say nothing of the misery they cause us.'

'Us? You, you mean. Flies don't bother me at all, nor Malcolm.' A snort of assent sounded behind my left shoulder. 'If you're at peace with yourself and the world around you, then the flies won't trouble you. It's as simple as that.'

Now I knew that Amanda was serious about the flies because I had heard from a woman who had once stayed at her house that she experienced similar tender feelings towards scorpions. Scorpions do not as a rule like water but for some reason they would come scuttling in from all corners of the surrounding country to fall into Amanda's pond and drown. So distressed was Amanda by this that she had a net prepared to fish out the poor mites, as she called them, and return them to the world of stones and scrub from whence they came.

My informant had good reason to be impressed by these actions. She had been stung on the mouth by one of Amanda's poor mites in bed. This was despite the fact that she was a woman at peace with herself and her surroundings, although naturally anyone would lose a certain amount of faith in their surroundings after an event like that. It did seem a shame that not all creatures shared Amanda's vision of the universe.

Amanda and Malcolm had arrived early for lunch and we had been showing them around Ana's vegetable patch. Ana edged the conversation tactfully away from our wanton slaughter of flies and onto the safer ground of natural fertilisers, as we prised Chloë from her sandpit and walked up to the house.

189

'Isn't it one of God's greatest miracles that the dung of the beasts carries all the elements essential to the growth of the plants that feed the very creatures that produce the manure that feeds the plants . . . and so on,' I rabbitted, anxious to display my organic credentials. 'The more I think of that particular fact, the more delighted I am by the organisation of the universe.'

'Being vegans, of course, we don't use animal manure,' Malcolm replied, 'only our own excreta – and seaweed.'

There was a pause.

'You're making a bit of a rod for your own back there, aren't you, Malcolm?' I suggested. 'I mean, importing seaweed when you're living in the mountains surrounded by copiously dunging animals?'

'Yes, it makes things much more difficult, of course, but we try not to use the products of any animal that is exploited. Animals should be wild and free like us.'

I looked hard at Malcolm. Wild and free were not the first two adjectives I would have hit upon.

'We don't wear leather shoes or woollen clothes, either.'

'Well, it certainly is a hard path you choose. But lunch must be ready now. Ana has prepared a meal that we hope will be acceptable in every way. It's amazing how you have to think to do it.'

Ana had indeed excelled herself. She presented us with a delicious-looking dish of aubergines, peppers, tomatoes, potatoes and garlic, all bubbling together in a spicy sauce of soya-milk yoghurt.

'I'm afraid we can't possibly eat that.'

'You what?!'

'We don't eat peppers or aubergines or tomatoes or potatoes. All those vegetables are *Solanaceae*, members of the deadly nightshade family. They're poisonous.'

'You'll enjoy the garlic then, just pick around the rest.'

190

～

The first thing you hear is a whistle that sounds like a tutubia, except that tutubias rarely come down to the river, preferring the scrub high in the hills. Then comes a rolling river of bells and you realise that it's Rodrigo calling to his goats. Up the river they come, in a dozen or more streams, picking their way over ledges and boulders or browsing by the water's edge while Rodrigo waits above the bank, keeping watch from beneath the brim of his ancient straw hat.

There's truth in what Amanda says about the destructive capacity of goats. Sheep are bad enough but goats are in a different league. A goat will stand on its back legs and reach eight feet in the air, ripping all the leaves and branches off the trees to that height. They are prodigious climbers and scramblers, sure-footed and fearless beyond belief, and their delicate pointed feet are like little jackhammers, scrabbling away earth banks, stone walls and the edges of terraces.

Kid, however, is delicious to eat, fetching a higher price than lamb, and on terrain where no other creature could survive, goats sustain themselves and produce a couple of litres of milk a day – not just ordinary milk, but milk with almost miraculous properties of healing and nourishment. So, in spite of the opposition of the ecologists there will always be goats and their goatherds in the Alpujarras.

I often walk across the lemon terrace and down the rocky ramp into the riverbed to pass the time of day with Rodrigo.

'Hola!' I greet him.

'Qué?' he asks.

That 'qué?' means 'what?', but not just an ordinary 'what?' It is delivered expansively, the head cocked, the palms upturned and stretched wide, and spoken loud and long. It means 'How are you doing? How's the wife and the little one? How's your life and

191

how is the farming and the crops?' I can't say it like Rodrigo does. It takes many years of walking with only goats and your own thoughts for company before you can manage the delivery of that particular 'qué'. I have to be more specific.

'How's your wife, Rodrigo?'

'Ay, Cristóbal, she's bad, very bad. She can hardly walk now, she's had a hard life.'

'I'm sorry to hear that.'

'You see, Cristóbal, life is but a breath. We come into this vale of sorrow, we're here four days, and if we get a chance to do some little good, do someone a favour, then we've done well and we can be a little happy perhaps. But then we're cut down and gone, just bones and dust. In truth we're no different from the dumb beasts, these goats I walk with.'

A pronouncement like this is best received in silence. I know Rodrigo well enough by now to respect the sincerity behind his awkward philosophising. Rodrigo has a truly generous spirit.

'I saw you talking with the Englishwomen yesterday. Were they saying things about me and the goats?'

'Well, mainly they were talking about the goats, Rodrigo. They don't like them at all, that's sure. It appears that they busy themselves out on the hill planting retama and then your goats come along and eat it.'

'Cristóbal, why would anyone want to plant retama in the *secano*? I can't see it.'

'It's strange, I know, but they say it is good for the soil – it stops the erosion. Anyway, I think they'd rather you didn't take your goats near their place.'

'There is a Via Pecuaria there and I have to pass it to get to the land above El Picacho. One is entitled to graze the Via Pecuaria. Look, Cristóbal, I don't want to be a bad neighbour to them – if they want to plant retama on the hill then that's fine with me, but there's not so much grazing about that I can afford to leave a *secano* like El Picacho. As the goats pass they will of course eat the young retama; it's only natural. You see my point?'

'I do, I do.'

And thus continues the endless battle between the ecologists and the pastoralists.

⁓

Rodrigo gets lonely in the river. He walks all day every day of the year with his goats, and he's done so in these mountains and valleys for fifty years. He has seen whole weather cycles change the face of his world. Years of drought when his pencil-thin animals had to scuff in the dust for the tiniest shoot – years when he needed all his herder's skill to seek out the places where, after months or even years without rain, some barely perceptible mist of moisture might remain. And years when for months at a time he couldn't get his horse across the swollen river, and had to go all the way down to the Seven-Eye bridge to get to his goat stable. Those were the easy years, he told me, when he could sit on a stone not a mile from his stable, with a couple of fertiliser bags tied over his head and shoulders – the preferred way of keeping off the lashing rain – and watch his goats gorge themselves.

Rodrigo had resigned himself to this harsh and lonely existence. It would never have occurred to him that one day his load might be lightened by someone to help – and least of all a frail-looking Dutch sculptress. But that's how it worked out.   193

Antonia, the Dutchwoman in question, had begun spending her summers at La Hoya, a crumbling farmhouse, just down the valley from El Valero. The day we met her, on her first summer in the valley, she had walked up the riverbed with her big smelly old dog and was trailing from terrace to terrace behind our ram, looking out from a wide-brimmed hat and moulding his shape in a lump of wax that she was working with her fingers.

'I'll separate him and shut him in for you if you like,' I offered. 'No, I prefer to watch him moving around with the flock. I get a more natural result that way.'

The ram seemed to take a dim view of being modelled, moving off as soon as Antonia got a good vantage, and leading her on a stumbling trail around the stony meadow. The business was further complicated by the heat of the day, because the wax kept melting, and every fifteen minutes or so Antonia had to dip it in the cooling water of the *acequia*. When she got back, of course, the flock had disappeared, and by the time she had found them the wax had started melting again. So I gave her a bucket which she filled with water and carried around with her.

By this method Antonia was able to make a certain amount of progress, and slowly the models took shape. She made a lot of sheep that summer, along with some bulls and goats – and a wonderful rendering of Domingo's donkey, Bottom. When she returned to Holland to cast some of her models in bronze, she left a little menagerie of wax figures in a drawer in our house, to the great delight of Chloë.

Rodrigo lives high above La Hoya at La Valenciana, about an hour and a half on horseback, but stables his goats at the lower farm. Each morning, having seen to the needs of the cows, the pigs, the chickens and the horse, he saddles up and moves off down the steep hill. Arriving at La Hoya, he ministers to any goats that need attention, then takes them out into the river or up onto the hills. Even in the scorching heat of summer he never takes a siesta; there'd be no time to fit it in. Goats don't mind the heat at all.

All of a sudden a slight variation appeared in the monotony of Rodrigo's existence. La Antonia, as he called her, took to walking with him in the river, occasionally fashioning an animal in wax as they progressed. Rodrigo must be the only goatherd in Spain with a model of a billy-goat cast personally for him in bronze;

it's an expensive process. When there was goatwork to be done, injections, wormings, washings and so on, Antonia would often spend the whole morning helping, and goatwork is a lot easier with two people than with one. On the odd occasion when it was necessary to put an animal out of its misery for one reason or another, Antonia would even kill goats for Rodrigo with a knife. Alpujarreños do not like to kill animals. I have to do the same on occasion for Domingo.

Antonia made a difference to Rodrigo's life, day to day, but when Rodrigo's wife, Carmen, fell ill and was rushed to hospital in Granada, her presence became vital. After shutting the goats in for the night, Antonia would drive Rodrigo home, help him tend to the other animals, then take him to Granada and stay there while he spent the whole night sitting beside his sick wife's bed. This is the custom here, the family is expected to deal with much of the nursing.

The vigil continued for nine days, and then Carmen came home, at least a little better. Since then La Antonia has become an adored honorary member of their family. When she goes to spend the night with them at La Valenciana it's only with the greatest reluctance that they let her go. I've never been inside Carmen and Rodrigo's home but Ana has. She went up there one day with Antonia and of course Carmen invited them in. It proved impossible to escape without eating and drinking all of the most delicious and precious consumable items in the house. Ana said it was like visiting with the queen.

Antonia spends long spells in Holland, earning money for her work in Spain, drumming up patronage and commissions, and doing the bronze castings for the figures she makes. When she leaves the valley on these trips, Rodrigo walks with his goats and weeps a little. 'I think God sent me the Antonia, Cristóbal,' he confided to me. While she's away he besieges us for news of her and judges minutely when a postcard might be expected.

Antonia is a real artist and she puts as much energy and artistry into her life as she does into her work. She gives and gives, and despite the fact that she's not very robust, nothing is too much trouble for her. And so life repays her, people love her. She's the only foreigner I know here who simply by being true to herself has become a part of the Alpujarra.

HERBS AND HUSBANDRY

IF WE HAD WORRIES ABOUT CHLOË – BEYOND HER SURVIVAL amid the scorpions and other terrors to infant life – it was that she might become lonely on an isolated farm with just her doting, middle-aged parents for company. She seemed happy enough consorting with the rude beasts that surrounded her, conducting scientific observations of the mole crickets and ants, and making the acquaintance of all the plants and shrubs that grew on the farm. But there are some games that can only be satisfactorily played with friends of the same species. Chloë, we knew, would sooner or later be needing a playmate. Luckily she found one – as close to hand as you can get at El Valero – in Rosa, Bernardo and Isabel's youngest daughter, 'given light' to a year before Chloë at their home in the farm across the river. From the day they met, Chloë and Rosa claimed one another as sisters and would keep themselves peacefully amused with such useful occupations as tossing cassette tapes into the lavatory or throwing stones at the sheep. Rosa couldn't speak English and, as Chloë hadn't a word of Dutch, they communicated in Spanish. Having a daughter who was a native Granadina and fluent in Spanish helped to contribute to our sense of being finally settled. 'You've sown your seed here – you're one of us now,' Old Man Domingo had told me.

Life was beginning to run more or less smoothly. We made enough money from the sheep, the seed-collecting and the shearing to get by and had begun to nurture plans to convert the disused house on the other side of the river near Domingo's house into a holiday cottage. Our home, while still far from opulent, was in good enough repair to keep the rain off in winter and the worst of the heat out in summer, while the farm was moving slowly towards some semblance of order and health. There was one blot, however, that was threatening to disturb the careful equilibrium that underpinned our domestic harmony. The dogs and the sheep were at war.

Bodger and Barkis had grown into a pair of massive but amiable mongrels. They were even bigger than the now full-grown Bonka, and in this, in the broad flatness of their noses and their bovine dispositions, I detected the hand of Rosa's dog, Cees, who had recently been sent to his maker after a grisly episode involving some chickens.

Bodger's ears had remained in the one-up-one-down configuration which left him as endearing as when he was a pup, and Barkis was also a beauty. Unfortunately Barkis was exceptionally dim. There wasn't an educable cluster of neurons in the whole of his thick skull, and he was an incorrigible chaser of sheep. Once he'd had a taste of the whole flock flying in panic up the hill, heads down and feet flailing madly in the dust, he couldn't resist; he had to make them repeat the performance every time he saw them. It drove me to distraction. No shepherd can allow such an abuse of their flock and after emerging from the house to find them yet again stranded on a nearby hillock, quivering with fear, I snapped.

'Right, that's enough, Ana. I'm going to shoot the bugger! Look, he's chased the sheep up the bloody hill again. They're terrified, the whole flock is a bundle of nerves.'

'Go on, give him one more chance, please.'

'I've given the sod chance after chance. I've been patient. I've been nice to him. I've shouted at him. I've whopped him. I've tried training him. But he's completely dim-witted. It's no use, he's got to go. I hate to do it because he's a lovely dog, but if I don't do something now he's going to start killing sheep, and I'm not having that.'

Ana and Chloë watched aghast as I stomped off across the valley to borrow Domingo's shotgun. My intentions were absolutely fixed. I was going to shoot that brainless cur and put an end once and for all to the terrorising of my sheep. But Domingo wasn't in, so I stomped back, secretly rather glad.

Trudging up the path to the terrace where we had buried Beaune, I came across Chloë, inexpertly digging with her sand spade. 'We'll have to bury Barkis, won't we, daddy?' she asked, gazing down with dread seriousness at the hamster-sized hole she'd just completed.

'No Chloë, I'm not going to shoot Barkis,' I answered, lifting her onto my shoulders, out of the way of scrutinising a face wracked with guilt. Ana was up at the house getting ready to visit all the dog-owners who might be persuaded to offer a home to Barkis. Janet promised to give the matter some thought.

Meanwhile, Barkis, oblivious of his reprieve, excelled himself by chasing the whole flock down the river to La Herradura, and then straight up the steep slope of La Serreta on the other side of the Cádiar river. I didn't see the wretched episode but Rodrigo the goatherd had watched the entire proceedings and had been decidedly unimpressed.

199

~

Manolo del Granadino broke the news of the exodus to me when I bumped into him later that day in town. He said he had seen the sheep grazing just above the almond groves of El Enjambre. There would be trouble if I didn't get them down as soon as possible, he reckoned.

'They'll come off the hill raiding at night and destroy all the vegetables of the *vega*, then you'll be for it.'

'I think you're being a little over-dramatic there, Manolo, but you're right, I'd better get up there and do something about it.' It was an odd notion, the idea of sheep as night-raiders, coming down like the Assyrian horde on the ranks of the valley farmers' vegetables . . . hiding in the inaccessible hills by day.

On the way back from town Ana drove me up to the Venta del Enjambre and left me there with a banana, a pinch of bread and a swig of water. I gathered up a stout stick and set off down the *barranco*, peering around for the sheep and straining my ears for the bells. It was a lovely, warm February afternoon, the sun veiled by thin cloud. I strolled down the track to La Hoya and stood by the river watching Ana and Chloë disappear round the hill and out of sight. No sign of the sheep, though. I doubled back the way I had come and after about ten minutes caught the distant bongling of bells. The flock was moving along the skyline, high above me. There was no way to get up to them from where I stood as the entire hill face was covered in chest-high gorse, so I changed direction and tramped eastwards in the hopes of finding a path.

Reaching the pass at the eastern end of the hill I had no option left but to pick my way downriver along the route by which I intended to bring the flock back. Still no path. Exasperated, I struck straight up the steep rock-toothed ridge, clambering on and on through the pine- and rosemary-scented air until, at last,

200

on the summit I discovered a feeble path, that seemingly started nowhere and ran along the ridge from peak to peak.

I sat down to regain my breath and, basking in the late afternoon sunshine, surveyed the scene below. Tiny El Valero was just visible to the trained eye, out beyond the river. Way off to the north were fields of snow shrouding the high peaks, with storm-clouds rolling around them; but where I was sitting was perfect peace, the rivers dimmed to a gentle sussuration, the odd tutubia skeetering away and screeching. I smiled to myself at the thought that the sheep had lured me up to this spot to allow me to enjoy an afternoon's ramble.

As if to crown the moment I heard the distant tinkle of sheep-bells. There they were, a mile off, tiny specks in the scrub, not far from where I'd seen them earlier. I struck down through the two hidden valleys with their tumbled fortifications – the Serreta had been a Republican redoubt during the last months of the Civil War – and across a long scree-slope waist-high with rose-mary. Creeping up, I remonstrated gently with my charges: 'This is no place for sheep, for heaven's sake! Goats maybe, but sheep, no. What on earth do you find to eat here anyway? There's not a stitch of grass.'

Looking around, I started wondering in earnest how I was going to get them down. They didn't want to go down, I could see that. 'Right, let's go home,' I said, and did a little clucking and whooping. Some of the sheep moved off rather unconvincingly in one direction.

201

I took stock of the situation. I didn't know where we were, nor did I know the lie of the land. Everywhere there were smaller or greater precipices, and with the waist-high scrub you couldn't see them until you were plunging headlong over. The sheep that I was about to throw a rock at, to get them to move along, could be teetering on the very edge of a sheer drop. I skirted around them to have a look. They were.

So with oaths and stones I turned them around and we headed steadily back along the hill the way I had come. It was hell getting them underway. 'Haaii!' I shouted, waving my stick, and a dozen sheep would move forward. The rest would look at them without much interest, then amble off down the hill, grazing as they went, so I hurtled down through the thorns and rocks to threaten the lower part of the flock. These moved off reluctantly in the right direction. Meanwhile the top lot had stopped and were heading higher up towards some nasty-looking rocks. I leaped back up again and headed them more or less in the right direction. Meanwhile, the lower part of the flock . . . I cursed myself for being fool enough not to have a proper sheepdog.

Still, by throwing stones and whooping and shouting, I managed to move them all onto the faintly discernible ridge path. As we picked our way gingerly along, I chatted to them to keep them relaxed and in a good mood. 'Just keep moving along there nicely now, girls. That's lovely, nice and steady now. Find your own way along, no hurry, plenty of daylight left,' and suchlike.

The views from that ridge were breathtaking but knowing that if I were to slip I would probably go hurtling over the edge somewhat dulled my appreciation. Luckily I have a fair head for heights, and the sheep, well, they leave such trivial worries to the shepherd. The leaders of the flock insisted on sticking slavishly to the exact ridge path, which meant climbing up to, and then clambering down from, the very pinnacle of every one of the jagged peaks of this saw-toothed little range. We must have cut a farcical figure from below as we moved along, silhouetted against the darkening sky.

With the setting of the sun, the full extent of my predicament began to dawn upon me. Here I was at the back, or sometimes in the middle, of a slowly moving flock of sheep, high on a precipitous mountaintop from which I had no clear idea of the way down. With the deepening shadows, the contours of the slopes

202

which had earlier filled me with such delight took on an increasing menace. If we reached the eastern end of the range, there was, as I well knew, no way down for a sheep. Even if I did manage to get them down to road level – and I could see the road, a fine grey ribbon far, far below, with tiny cars and lorries whispering along it – I would somehow have to turn them towards the river, and away from the lush vegetable fields of the *vega* at the bottom. No easy feat for one exhausted shepherd. I would just have to leave the whole thing to chance.

The sun sank lower, black clouds fouled the sky, the night drew deeper and the sheep ambled along ever more slowly. My thoughts were by now of the blackest. The plants I had enjoyed earlier plucked spitefully at me as I passed, while rocks seemed to shoot from the ground to wrack my ankles.

'We ought to cut down to the right here,' I announced to the sheep, 'because although it looks a hellish descent, it's certainly a lot easier than the face at the end – and whatever you do, sheep, don't you even think about the north side! That way lies despair.' The urge to talk aloud at that fearful moment, even to sheep, was irresistible.

The sheep didn't much like the look of the north side either. It was an awesome prospect of steep rocky slopes, covered in thick scrub, with cliffs that plunged hundreds of feet to the river. Running through the bushes on their left flank, I redoubled my efforts, hurling rocks and yelling like a banshee. 'Down there – down there, you stupid buggers. Look, I know it looks grim, but take my word for it, it's a lot less bloody grim than what's ahead of you if you keep on along that ridge!' They looked at me, chewing insolently, and moved on straight up the edge of the next, last and highest peak.

'Bloody Nora! You brainless shits – look at the mess you've got us into now! How in the name of Beelzebub are we going to get down off this?' The cars spinning silently along the road below

203

had their lights on now. A quarter moon sailed among the threatening clouds.

As I moved round, stumbling across the north side of the peak, the sheep at the back turned quietly round and trotted off back the way we had just come. I stopped and stared after them in horror. A Sisyphean vision swam into view of an eternity of walking back and forth along the skyline of this ridge with my dim-witted animals. The flock was fragmenting little by little, some moving back the way we had come, some thinking about the north face, one or two eating on the slope I wanted them to go down, but most of them just standing and looking thoughtfully into the gathering night.

I tried one final burst of frenzied activity, leaping back and forth over the ankle-cracking rocks in the dark, howling and yelling and thrashing the scrub with my stick. It was no good. I had to admit defeat for the night, anyway, and slithered off down that horrible slope.

As I went I made the noises favoured by local people who want sheep to follow them. The sheep listened courteously but decided against it. And fifty metres down the hill I came across the path I had been looking for on the way up.

∾

204 The next day Domingo and Antonio offered to come up with me to get the sheep off the hill. 'That's very good of you,' I said. 'But I really can't see how we're going to get them down.'

We headed up the hill armed with Domingo's pack of five nondescript curs, and after about an hour's scramble managed to locate the sheep, more or less where I had left them, at the top of the steep cliffs.

'We'll push them down the north side,' said Domingo. 'They'll always go down best the way they came up.'

'You're joking, Domingo. That side is about ninety percent vertical cliff.'

Antonio rolled a cigarette and kept his own counsel.

'Bah!' said Domingo and whistled the bird whistle he uses to get his flock moving. The sheep raised their heads, startled. Then they bolted as one, straight over the edge of the cliff.

I rushed panic-stricken to the edge, expecting to see their little woolly bodies plummeting hundreds of feet through the air to shatter on the rocks of the river far below. But no, there they were, skittering from ledge to ledge, bum up, ears down, hurtling headlong down that impossible hill. It took them seven and a half minutes to reach the river, and then they shot up to the farm and in minutes were lost to view on the orange terraces.

'Well, that wasn't very difficult!' said Domingo brightly, as we all sat down on a rock to look at the view and enjoy the smoke curling away from Antonio.

~

No sooner had the news reached Janet about the Serreta incident than she came striding across the valley to see us. 'Out of my way! There's a dog's life at stake!' she shouted at some hikers who coincided with her at the bridge.

'I've found an excellent position for Barkis,' she announced when she reached the house. 'Good European family,' she added, meaning they weren't Spanish. 'Now, how much does the dog weigh? The people I've found are very concerned that he should not weigh more than twenty kilos. They don't want to be pulled over by him. How much? Thirty kilos? Well, that should be alright. He's a beautiful boy, just right for them. I'll ring them tonight. They'll be down to collect him tomorrow.'

The dogs happened to be suffering from fleas at the time; there was an outbreak in the stable by the workshop where Bodger

205

and Barkis had their quarters. We covered them all with flea-powder that night, in the hope that they might look more presentable the following day.

As Janet had promised, Barkis's prospective owners turned up next morning, equipped with a pair of bathroom scales. The flea-powder had done its work and brought all the fleas biting furiously to the surface of the dogs' coats. So the dogs were twisting and turning and scratching and gnawing at themselves in a frenzy of itching. You could actually see the wretched fleas hopping. Nevertheless, Barkis could turn on the charm when he thought it might be in his interest to do so. George and Alison were so delighted by him that they took him home with them that very night.

Barkis fell on his feet with his new owners. They have a rabbit farm and they supplemented his diet with dead rabbits. They also took him for walks on their mountain every day and to church with them on Sundays. He thrived under this tender regime and gave up chasing sheep altogether. Then he was poisoned by the hunters.

Hunters in the Alpujarras routinely put poisoned bait down to kill any beast that might disturb their birds. It's a highly illegal as well as cruel practice and a lot of dogs die horrible deaths as a result. But few of the victims' owners bother to make any sort of fuss. Not so George and Alison. They were wretched with misery when Mariano the shepherd brought them their dog, dead in his arms, and immediately launched a campaign to publicise the outrage. The mayor was petitioned, legal advice was sought regarding criminal proceedings, and together with the village pharmacist they produced an emetic to distribute free of charge to anyone whose dog was in danger. It was a shame that Barkis couldn't have witnessed his ascension to cause célèbre.

206

~

If the truth be told, Barkis was not the only one of our dogs liable to kill sheep. All dogs will have a go at chasing sheep given the opportunity, but some more so than others. One summer morning the sheep strayed onto a terrace uncomfortably close to Ana's vegetable patch. I ran down to move them off, and the dogs followed. Bonka stood eagerly by as I pushed the flock through the gate. Bodger, however, was not to be found. Fearing the worst I raced up to the far end of the terrace – and there came upon a grisly scene. A sheep was stuck in the mesh fence, and was struggling helplessly while Bodger was methodically tearing it to pieces.

I yelled at the dog, heaved a huge rock, and missed. Then I disentangled what was left of the poor creature from the fence. She stood, swayed a little and collapsed in a pool of blood. I rolled her over to have a look at her wounds, averting my eyes and sucking a long breath through my teeth until the spasm of horror passed. I didn't know just what fearful wounds those teeth could inflict. The sheep's legs, back and front, were torn apart, like cut meat on a butcher's slab. Her belly was ripped deep and there were bloody toothmarks all over her.

I had never seen such a horrible savaging and ran up to the house to get a knife to finish her off. But when I got back she had heaved herself to her feet and was staggering towards the stable.

'If she has that much will to live,' said Ana, 'then it would be wrong to put her down. We must try and treat her.'

'Have you seen the wounds, Ana? They are appalling, she can't possibly survive.'

'We can try, anyway. I'll consult Juliette.' And so saying, she retreated to the house to pore over *The Complete Herbal Handbook for Farm and Stable* by Juliette de Baïracli-Levy, which lay permanently to hand on the corner of our kitchen table.

I helped the sheep to the stable, made her a pen bedded with fresh straw, and put her lamb in with her. Though she must have

207

been suffering unimaginable pain, the first thing she did was to haul herself to her feet to let the lamb drink. This was definitely a sheep worth saving. I gave her an injection of antibiotics and a feed. Ana came down with some sort of natural cleansing solution, as recommended by Juliette, and bathed the wounds carefully as I held the sheep. She washed away every speck of dirt from every wound on the body, pulling away the wool where it had stuck to the meat.

I couldn't bear to look at the wounds – the sight of that torn flesh made my blood crawl – but Ana set to work with patience and skill. It took two hours just to clean the wounds. Then we fitted loose bandages wherever possible to keep off the thousands of flies intent on debauching themselves on her blood.

The next morning, as prescribed by Juliette, I had to urinate first thing in a bucket, the resultant liquid to be used for the bathing of wounds. Ana and I walked down to the stable (me rather self-consciously swinging the bucket) and tipped the sheep over to remove its bandages. The wounds were now covered in scabs and clots and bits of straw but the sheep munched contentedly while Ana doused them with my morning pee. And so we proceeded, for a week or so, administering one or other ghastly herbal drench from Juliette's natural animal husbandry regime, as the ewe visibly recovered. It kept milking throughout, and its lamb thrived.

208   Apart from one tendon – whose tear would have needed microsurgery beyond Juliette's primer and which left a bent forefoot – the sheep recovered completely. She has reared two sets of twins since and the long period of treatment made her quite tame.

It was a result that went beyond the benefits of a single sheep. Knowing that we had rescued the animal, and treated her with natural medicines, left me feeling quite different about my flock and indeed the whole style of farming we were able to practise.

In a big efficient flock, sheep with a far better chance of survival than this one would have been knocked straight on the head.

As for Bodger, well – we kept a careful eye on him after that.

~

Over the years, Juliette de Baïracli-Levy has attained such an influence over our household that it's hard not to think of her as a resident in-law, one of a triad of women who dictate the course of my life. She stayed down the road in Lanjarón during the 1950s, and was, or still is (for rumour has it that she lives today among a clump of pine trees on Mount Hermon, a somewhat contentious spot on the borders of Israel, Syria and Lebanon), a woman obsessed with herbs and natural ways of healing. One of her claims to fame is that, during her time in Spain, she nursed herself and her four-year-old son through typhus, pitting herself against the Lanjarón doctors by insisting on following her own prescriptions of herbs and fresh water.

A battered, second-hand copy of *Spanish Mountain Life*, Juliette's wonderfully quirky and triumphant account of that year in Lanjarón, formed our introduction to her works. Then some friends sent us a copy of *The Complete Herbal Handbook for Farm and Stable*. On the back were all sorts of testimonials from no-nonsense bodies like the British Horse Society and *Farmers' Weekly*. Juliette was thus stamped with the mark of respectability. 209

On many an evening when I came home tired and dusty from the field or the hill, I would find Ana engrossed in the more worryingly entitled *Illustrated Herbal Handbook for Everyone*, soon to be dubbed 'Towards a Healthier and More Wholesome Husband through Herbs'. Ana would regard me pensively as she looked up from the pages. Then, to her undisguised delight, I whacked the sharp point of a sickle into the side of my knee as I was clearing an *acequia* channel. This is a typical Alpujarran wound, by all accounts, all men having been born with a sickle in their hand and most of them subsequently going on one way or another to get it in their knee. Mine went in deep, and the knee swelled up like a football.

Ana consulted Juliette, then made a poultice of herbs and a vile potion that I was to drink. Comfrey was an ingredient of both poultice and potion, and the drink also featured coarse wormwood and garlic, just in case I should not find it sufficiently detestable. I'm more or less convinced that it worked, for the wound healed unusually fast. Meanwhile, Ana's confidence in her powers as a herbal healer soared. She could hardly wait for another opportunity to test her new skill.

Not long after the business with the knee, I obliged her by being very sick indeed. Ana found me vomiting violently into the rosebushes one afternoon, wishing to die. She sat down on a stone beside me and leafed through the wretched book. 'Juliette says here that it's a wonder that man is so concerned to stop vomiting which is a natural and wholesome purge for all the ills of the body. What do you think of that, eh?'

'BAAUUUGGHHH!'

'But if you really do feel as bad as you look, then you can have some grated raw quince, some cloves, ginger and lemon juice. That'll fix you up.'

210   It did, given time, and a reluctance to repeat the cure.

∼

Juliette's record with us remains good so far, and at El Valero her dictums are applied equally to humans, sheep, horses, dogs and cats – the last being surprisingly accommodating. I am always amused to watch them eagerly queuing up for their weekly dose of garlic, honey and wormwood balls, while at full moon Bonka and Bodger get pomegranate juice and garlic for their worms. Even Ana, however, stops short at embracing all Juliette's ideas, for it must be said that there is a puritanical streak in the books.

Juliette disapproves strongly, for example, of what she calls 'fired food' – that is to say cooked food – which she claims destroys the ingredients' natural goodness and healthful properties. Nor, she says, should you wear rubber-soled shoes, as they deny you the benefits of the wholesome natural emanations of the earth. Still, Juliette is always worth consulting on the less obvious problems that might beset one – how to deal, for example, with the rotting carcasses that are apt to appear in one's garden.

At El Valero, when a sheep dies of mysterious causes and so cannot be consigned to the pot, it gets bundled into a wheelbarrow and heaved over the *barranco*. The dogs watch this performance with ill-feigned indifference. They string the thing out for a couple of days, until the sheep starts to develop an interesting flavour, then they start work on it. Over the next ten days or so, the sheep returns to haunt us in the form of foul-smelling meaty limbs torn from the carcass and great wodges of rotting flesh with wool on it. The dogs bring these up to the house and spread them around the garden. It's not a practice to everybody's taste.

When things get really bad, these offerings start to make their presence felt in the house itself. One night I stepped out of bed in the dark and found myself treading on something large, sharp and slimy. With a squeal I lunged for the torch and discovered the skull of a wild boar, with some interesting bits of flesh still clinging to it. The dogs, who had found it in the river, stood proudly by wagging their tails.

Ana consulted Juliette, who was of course very much in favour of unfired flesh for the dogs, and somewhat dismissive of our objections to the smell of the stuff lying around the house and garden. Why, it might even have the beneficial effect of bringing

211

on a healthy bout of vomiting. She did, however, have a solution that would not only keep the dead animals out of harm's way but would provide a cheap store of dog food. It involved boning the meat and then burying it beneath a mat of selected herbs which were to preserve it.

As the man of the house, I was delegated to dig the hole. It was a hot summer day and the earth was like concrete. I cursed Juliette roundly as I picked and scrabbled about under Ana's supervision. 'That's quite deep enough now,' I grumbled.

'It's not. Juliette says it should be a good metre deep.'

'Juliette wouldn't have had to dig the damn hole.'

'No, she would very sensibly have got some man to do it for her. It wants to be a lot deeper than that . . . and finish the sides off nicely. I'm going to gather herbs.'

When she returned from the herb-gathering, Ana looked disdainfully at the hole. It wasn't as Juliette had ordained but it would have to do. Ana and Chloë watched from a safe distance while I boned the meat. You don't do jobs like this in summer, and for a very good reason. I worked in a cloud of flies and wasps. It's not pleasant having two or three dozen wasps wandering about on your hands, but fortunately they were too engorged in blood and meat to care much about stinging.

Soon I was left with a couple of buckets full of glistening meat, black with flies and wasps. I rinsed it carefully under the tap to wash off the flies' eggs. Ana meanwhile had exerted herself and laid a mat of herbs of one sort or another in the hole.

'Place the meat on the mat of herbs, then I'll lay some rosemary, lemon thyme, southernwood and rue on top.'

'That sounds like the same ingredients you give the dogs to worm them – and just about everything else too.'

'Well, whatever the recipe, it's supposed to preserve the meat and all its nourishing qualities for at least three months, and to protect it from insect attack. I'm sure it's the answer.'

She placed the herbs on the meat in the hole. 'Now you must place heavy stones on top to stop the wild creatures digging it up, it says here, and then fill the hole in.'

You can imagine our excitement when, six weeks later, the time came to exhume the preserved meat and feed it to the dogs. I cleared the earth away and then heaved the stones from the hole. There lay the protective herb matting, miraculously intact. It soon became apparent though, as we lifted the layer of herbs, that there was no meat inside. It had vanished without trace, not a stain, nor a shred, nor a particle of flesh remained. The hole was perfectly undisturbed, not even so much as a scrabble mark. We all stood and gaped in bafflement at the empty hole with its useful herbal matting.

'Where's it gone, Daddy?' asked Chloë with a touching faith that I was somehow lurking at the bottom of this mystery.

'I don't know, Chloë. I thought you might have come and gobbled it up in the night.'

'EEEyuk,' she squealed, running behind some bushes as if to hide from the thought.

'Well, that was certainly a useful exercise. I can't wait till the next sheep drops dead so we can do it again.'

'Mmm,' said Ana. 'You win some, you lose some, and being facetious won't make a blind bit of difference.'

We haven't repeated the meat-preserving recipe; it doesn't seem like time well spent and I rather like the thought of keep- 213 ing one notable failure up my sleeve to throw back at Juliette should her rule prove too tyrannical. As for the rotting bones on the terrace, we just garden round them now.

MARKET FORCES

ONE EVENING AFTER A LONG DAY'S SHEARING, DOMINGO AND
I and a gang of high sierra shepherds were sitting in Ernesto's
Bar in the woods below Pampaneira, eating tapas of meat from
the grill – *carne a la brasa* – and doing some earnest *costa* tast-
ing. The conversation had turned to how much we all loved our
ganado: our flocks. Odd though it may seem, this is a fairly popular topic of conversation hereabouts.

As the shepherds droned eloquently on about their feelings
for their charges, I noticed Ernesto's son watching me. He was
fairly well gone and seemed to be plucking up the courage to ask
me a question. Finally on his way back from the bar he lurched
towards me and whispered breathily in my ear, 'Do you too love
the *ganado*?' 'I cannot deny it but I do,' I whispered in reply, and
we smiled bashfully at one another.

Domingo caught the undertone. 'What do you mean?' he inter-
rupted. 'You don't even know your own sheep. When did you last
walk with them? You've been putting up fences to do your job

214

for you. Those sheep of yours wouldn't even follow you if you wanted them to. That's not loving the *ganado*.'

These were wounding words, but I couldn't deny that there was a certain truth in them. Since the fiasco of the lost flock I had been busy erecting fences over a large swathe of the *secano* precisely so that I could shrug off the more wearisome duties of the shepherd and get on with more pressing jobs on the farm. Also neither I nor the sheep had quite mastered the easy technique of the Alpujarran shepherd who strides at the head of a flock, whistling for the sheep to follow. Instead I would be left bringing up the rear, shouting and pitching stones. It wasn't the most flattering comparison. My sheep were in good condition, well kept and produced a good number of lambs, but then no one was criticising my sheep. I shrank back under these mortifying reflections and waited for Domingo's show of pique to pass and for the conversation to turn to other matters.

Soon enough the tender eulogising of sheep had shifted into an angry tirade against the dealers. Everyone, it seemed, had fared badly at the last round of selling and all were swearing to hold out for a better price next time.

'I don't see why we should bother with the dealers at all,' I piped up. 'We can't do worse than we're doing now if we cut out the middle man and sell our lambs ourselves.' It was a bold outburst in such company but I rather enjoyed the lull it created in the conversation. 'When the dealers get a knockdown price they take the lambs to Baza to turn over a quick profit,' I continued recklessly, 'so why shouldn't we try our luck selling direct? I know I'm going to give it a go.' A few seconds before I hadn't known anything of the sort but the looks of startled interest on the faces around me had transformed the vague idea that had been hovering at the back of my mind into a one-man mission. It felt good to be back in the role of innovator again.

Baza market is the largest livestock market in Andalucía, set on a high plateau about three hours' drive away in the north of the province. The dealers who frequent it are a hard-bitten crowd and trying to offload lambs direct would be tricky and contentious even without the handicap of being a foreigner and a relative novice to the trade. But I couldn't back out now.

'The dealers won't like it a bit,' announced one of the shepherds, his eyes glinting with excitement at the thought. 'No,' said another, 'but it's something that's got to come, they can't go on screwing us for ever.'

'Well, the dealers can look after themselves,' I replied. 'I've got forty good lambs that are ready to go. Does anyone want to come with me?'

Perhaps I hadn't phrased the question clearly enough because the debate raged on in abstract terms without anyone actually answering it. Domingo's voice, however, eventually cut through the bluster. 'I'll come with you,' he said. 'You have a word with Baltasar about his trailer. We can give it a try at the market a week tomorrow.'

~

Baltasar, one of my sheep-shearing cronies, has a powerful four-wheel-drive truck and a livestock trailer. He agreed to take us to Baza Market because he needed to stock up on hay-racks and things for his flock. So, on a sharp winter's evening, we loaded the lambs into the trailer and, as a counterweight, stuffed the car with various people who had decided to come along for the ride. Baltasar drove; then there was Domingo and his cousin Kiki, a lad I'd not met before, for the good reason that he was just out of jail for an episode involving a sawn-off shotgun and a discotheque; and lastly Baltasar's father, Manuel. Naturally I was stumping up for the expedition.

216

We set off in a leisurely fashion at about nine o'clock in order to get to the market at midnight. This was some unfathomable notion of Domingo's. The market started at six in the morning but Domingo reckoned it was best to get there before the rush started; midnight seemed a bit excessive to everybody else but Domingo was adamant. In the event, as ever, it took a while to get away. As we passed through Órgiva we were flagged down for a chat by every passer-by who happened to know Domingo or Baltasar, or anyone who was simply curious about the trailerload of lambs. By the time we finally left the town it seemed that all its inhabitants knew of my madcap plan to sidestep the local dealers and sell the lambs direct at Baza market.

The same thing happened in Lanjarón, Baltasar's home town, but at last we were away, leaving the mountain roads of the Alpujarra and grumbling slowly up the long hills that lead to Granada. The cool evening had become a freezing night, so the heater was on and the car was full of soporific fug. Soon everyone was asleep except Baltasar, Manuel and me. Baltasar was awake because he was driving, Manuel was awake because he was holding forth in an unbroken narrative, and I was awake because I was too polite to go to sleep when someone was talking to me. The others had heard it all before.

Manuel is a *curandero* – something between a faith healer and a barefoot doctor. His speciality is bones, muscles and the nervous system. He is known throughout Andalucía and I have heard of his successes from Málaga to Jaén. He is a fine-looking man with a bearing of unpretentious dignity, and despite his tiny frame he possesses an almost supernatural strength as well as a limitless capacity for talking. He sat in front with Baltasar. It was his car, so he was accorded that dignity, although he never would presume to try and drive the thing. Like reading and writing, driving is the province of a younger, more advanced, technologically literate class of person.

217

As he spoke he twisted round in the tall seat to address me and make sure I was still listening. 'Well yes,' he explained when I broke the monologue with a question. 'There was a doctor in the town shortly after the war, and he didn't like me practising at all. He made life as difficult as he could, got the Guardia Civil to harass us: he was friends with the town *comandante*. The church doesn't like *curanderos*, you see, and the doctor, as well as being a second-rate practitioner who only attended the needs of the rich people of the town (and that badly) the doctor was a very churchy man. So I could only practise with the greatest difficulty. One winter, the Guardia locked me up in the town jail for three weeks – no heating and not enough to eat – and gave me a thorough beating, too.'

'But it didn't make you want to give up the healing?'

'No, it's a gift, the healing. Like the gifts of sight or hearing it's hard to stop using them. People come to me with their pains and their sicknesses and I know I can help them. So I do; I can't help it. I don't take any money for it, only what people want to give, but I do get an awful lot of pleasure from it.

'Anyway, late one night there was a knock at the door. When I opened it I found a woman wrapped from head to foot in a dark blanket. I led her in to the light, and as I turned to look at her I understood why she had covered herself so. She was the wife of the *comandante*. She told me she was in great pain with her legs; she hadn't slept for weeks from the pain and the doctor had told her there was nothing he could do.

218

'I soon discovered what was wrong with her; it was trapped nerves, the poor woman could hardly walk. I treated her several times during the course of the week – she always came at night and hidden, it wouldn't do for the wife of the *comandante* to be seen consorting with *curanderos* – and at the end of the week she was completely better, not a trace of pain. From then on I never had any more trouble with the Guardia.'

Manuel's stories were too good to doze through. He told them well, fluently and with a fine sense of balance and dramatic timing. Those who cannot read or write have the advantage in this; the ability to keep a long story in one's head tends to diminish with literacy.

He launched into another story about what happened to the doctor – of course he got his come-uppance – and I had no doubt that the story was true. Then he moved on to a tale about another doctor. Various people of the town, the butcher Sevillano, the baker, the café owner who had been nursed by a donkey, all wandered in and out of the narrative. He kept up non-stop, wriggling round every few minutes to see that I was still listening. I crouched forward to catch his quiet voice above the thrum of the engine and rumbling of the trailer.

As we turned east and ground up towards the Puerto del Lobo, I realised that the monologue had shifted into new territory. The workaday world he described was being infiltrated by new and unlikely characters. A fisherman appeared on the scene. Lanjarón is high in the mountains and twenty miles inland; one thing it does not have is a fishing fleet. Then came elements that seemed somehow strangely familiar. With some surprise I realised that Manuel had moved seamlessly into the Tales of the Arabian Nights. The jealous doctor and the venal priests were soon eclipsed by a procession of princes and djinns and viziers and sages.

219

~

We swung through the main gate of the market not long after midnight.

'You're the first here,' said the half-frozen man in the gatehouse. 'Five hundred pesetas and you can have a pen right at the top, best position of all.'

'Marvellous,' I said, handing over the money. 'Good thing, getting here early.' Baltasar grunted. Everyone else was fast asleep.

We pulled across the empty concrete plain of the market yard and stopped by the top row of pens. Baltasar switched off the engine, stretched and groaned. I opened the door to get out and stretch my legs – and immediately closed it again. I didn't know Spain got this cold. It wasn't till I read the next day's paper, which quotes Baza as one of the extremes of temperature for Andalucía, that I found out that it was ten degrees below zero.

Apparently the human body gives off the equivalent of a kilowatt of heat, so five of us ought to have heated up that car like a steam-bath. It didn't work. Everyone was awake within five minutes, teeth chattering, squirming this way and that, unbearably uncomfortable. 'Surely there's a bar or somewhere where we can go and sit in the warm?'

'Not till later.'

'Run the engine then, for heaven's sake, man!'

'Not now, I can't keep it running all morning.'

~

At four o'clock the bar opened. It was ten degrees below outside; it was ten degrees below inside. The bar was a huge, stone-floored, white, neon-lit shed designed to be cool on hot summer mornings. We left the door open; there didn't seem to be much point in shutting it. The bartender came in, shivering and complaining bitterly. We drank brandies to occupy ourselves while the coffee machine got up steam. The barman went out and returned with some olive logs with which he lit a barbecue in the corner by the kitchen door. We all edged towards it. A couple of girls stumbled in, just out of deep sleep and marginally on the right side of hypothermia. They stood by the now blazing barbecue and surveyed the customers with indifference.

At around four-thirty others started to dribble in. Heavily-swaddled lorry drivers and shepherds. A dealer, noisy in a sharp suit and quilted anorak, holding forth to his entourage of toadies. A short man in a leather jacket and beret limped in and sat on a chair near the fire.

'You've got a nasty limp there!' said Manuel enthusiastically.

The beret looked at him in astonishment, for although it is the custom in Spain not to deny people their afflictions, it's not usually done quite so directly. 'It is a nasty limp,' he said slowly. 'And what's it to you?'

'I take an interest in such afflictions. I make them better. What's wrong with the leg?'

'Well, they're both bad, been like it for twenty years now. The doctors say it comes from the cold on these mountains and they can't do anything about it.'

'Can you straighten them both out like that?'

'No.'

'Bend them like this?'

'No, not that way either.'

'What you need is to do exercises. I do them every day, and look at me; the cold hasn't even got to me yet.'

This was not an empty boast since Baltasar's family have the highest farm on the mountain above Lanjarón, a spot that enjoys truly gargantuan weather, and Manuel has spent most of his life working there. But the man in the beret looked dubious. He wouldn't do the exercises, I could see that. He hobbled off to get another brandy. Manuel set off to do a tour of the bar and see what other interesting afflictions he could find. 221

Domingo and I, leaving Baltasar to watch out for Kiki and make sure he didn't pull some stunt in the market bar, went to pen up the lambs and cast an eye over the opposition. Our pen seemed to be a long way from all the others. The action, such as it was, was taking place at the bottom end of the market. Here there were larger lots of lambs, a hundred, two hundred to a pen. My forty lambs were good, but a little smaller than most, and the fact of their being huddled up in a corner of the pen didn't show them off to their best advantage.

In the pen next to mine was a mixed bag of old goats, and on the other side a smelly billygoat milling about amongst a small bunch of ill-favoured lambs. Apart from us, all the other pens up our end were empty. It didn't take a lot of thought to work out that this was where they put the punters who didn't know the ropes. My neighbours were certainly not out of the top drawer of modern-thinking shepherds.

My five hundred pesetas had rented a concrete pen beneath a huge open shed. Here I displayed my wares to their best advantage, leaning on the door nonchalantly as if it were a matter of complete indifference whether I sold them or not. The dealers moved around the pens with an entourage of note-takers, purveyors of unsolicited advice, toadies and desperate shepherds. The vendors made their own deals with the buyers on the basis of whatever information they could pick up by listening in to the dealing at the other pens.

By six, the lower end of the market was seething with activity. It was the darkest and coldest hour of the night. I thought I had dressed warmly but it wasn't enough for this. Frozen solid from my toes to my ears, I could hardly talk – I certainly couldn't get my mouth around sheep-dealing Andaluz. Domingo wandered up from the pens below.

222

'Bad news, the prices are getting lower. One of the shepherds in the big pens down there has just accepted seven thousand and his lambs are the biggest and best here. Smaller lambs are going for nothing. Also Luís Vazquez is down there and unless I'm much mistaken he has spread the word that nobody should take any interest in your lambs.'

'Why ever not?'

'He was angry because you didn't sell him your lambs when he came to see you . . . '

'Of course I didn't, not at the ridiculous price he was offering!'

'Well anyway, he and the other dealers of the Alpujarras are not pleased with the prospect of more shepherds bringing their own lambs to market. It'll put them out of business.'

'Good thing too.'

'Yes, but they're not going to take it lying down. Luís has been talking to all the dealers here in the market. They'll want to teach us all a lesson.'

Occasionally, as if to lend weight to Domingo's words, a dealer and his entourage would break away from the melee at the lower end of the market and saunter up past my pen, look at the lambs with a sneer and pass on without a word. Domingo did his best to engage them in conversation and draw attention to the advantages of my lambs, but to no avail.

I leaned forlornly on the wall, looking at the poor frightened creatures in the pen. How much longer would this ghastly ordeal go on? Everywhere I could see batches of lambs being shoved down the corridors to the loading-bays. Fat-bellied dealers were climbing into their Mercedes and sweeping away through the gates. It looked like I would have to endure the humiliation of taking the lambs home again, a wretched double journey as well as a night of cold and misery for them.

'We won't go yet, though,' said Domingo. 'It often happens that prices get better towards the end of the market. Perhaps some dealers won't have made up their quota and there'll be fewer lambs to choose from. We may be lucky yet!'

We weren't. The spasm of buying and selling had climaxed and ebbed. A feeble white sun crept up from behind the horizon and illuminated that horrid place with rays devoid of warmth. The big pens of lambs emptied and the big dealers disappeared one by one. In the carpark beside the shed, the village dealers and

223

small-time operators cruised up and down the lines where those too canny to pay the five hundred pesetas for a pen plied their wares. Here were battered Renault 4s, their windows steamed with the breath of a dozen lambs, a goat trussed up and lashed to the back of a tractor, an old man standing forlornly with a couple of thin sheep on a rope. But nobody came even to look at my lambs. I felt lost and lonely, like a new boy at school.

I had a coffee with Baltasar, leaving Domingo to try and drum up some interest among the remaining buyers.

'It doesn't look like you're going to sell them today.'

'Yes, I suppose I'll have to take them home again.'

'You should be a little careful, you know; you've made some enemies among the dealers, and they're bad people to cross. You never know what they might try, not in broad daylight like this but on a dark night on a lonely mountain road . . .'

He left the sentence unfinished. I thought he was being a little dramatic, but maybe it was serious. I was breaking the mould, sticking my neck out. It was a foolhardy failure. We loaded up the lambs again and headed for home. As we passed through Lanjarón and Órgiva we made frequent stops to satisfy the curiosity of passers-by. Some of them had already spoken to the dealers and they seemed to know already the minutest detail of our humiliating journey.

224   ~

Predictably enough there was a flurry of interest among the dealers to see if they could get the unsold lambs for nothing. I would have to sell them; it wouldn't be long before they went past their best, and then I really would have to give them away. The man who gave me the most reasonable deal was a gypsy from Órgiva called Francisco. He was such a small operator that he hadn't the wherewithal to go to the market in Baza. Domingo told me to watch him, as he was known to be a bad payer, but he paid me in advance as he took the lambs away in four batches of ten over the next month.

I have sold to Francisco ever since, and so far he has not let me down. Now I've come to like selling the lambs locally. It's by far the most ecological option; it saves the lambs a stressful journey, saves on transport costs, and it pleases me to be supplying the community in which we live. Occasionally people will come up to me and compliment me on the quality of lamb they buy at Francisco's stall in the market. Francisco himself is a firm believer in the superior quality of *carne campero*.

'No, this bringing the lambs up on high-protein feed in the dark is a modern notion. In my father's time as a butcher, a lamb wasn't considered fit to eat until it had grazed for a summer in the high pasture. The lambs were bigger and older then but the flavour was superb. My older customers complain that they can't get any good meat any more. The stuff they buy just shrivels to nothing in the pan. So I'm really pleased to see you producing *carne campero*. I'll buy whatever you produce.'

It was no October Revolution, leading the shepherds of the Alpujarras to cast away their chains, but for me, perhaps, things had turned out again for the best.

CHLOË'S CHRISTENING

WHEN CHLOË WAS BORN WE PLANNED A PARTY TO CELEBRATE her arrival and thought we might combine it with a christening. Ana, having spent some of her school years at a convent, was convinced of the importance of baptism. I live in a state of confusion about the mysteries of the universe and was not so sure, but there was one advantage to having a christening that settled my doubts. We could ask Domingo to be Chloë's godfather.

Domingo is the sort of friend who hates to be thanked for anything. He carries his generosity lightly and dismisses the time and energy he unstintingly gives us as not worth mentioning. If I try to press the issue he grows brusque and severe. So to have a formal token at hand, one that would imply our appreciation and regard, was just too good an opportunity to be missed. I raised the godfather business with him the very day that we decided one might be necessary.

'What do I have to do?' he asked doubtfully.

226

'Well, not much. I think you just hold Chloë when the priest splashes the water.'

'I might just about manage that.'

'And then of course you have to see to her spiritual upbringing.'

'I'll be good at that too,' he grinned.

'Well then, will you do it?'

'I don't mind,' he said, seeming to mull it over. 'That's if I'm not doing anything else on that day.'

Domingo certainly knows how to take the wind from your sails. Still, he was clearly pleased with the idea, and Expira and Old Man Domingo were delighted. So, having sown the seeds, I set about bringing our plan to fruition. The first thing to do was to seek out the parish priest.

~

Don Manuel was usually to be found, outside the hours of Mass or siesta, in a murky little office beside the church. His house-keeper opened the door with a broom in her hand and on hearing my mission ushered me into his presence. He stopped shuffling the papers around his desk and got to his feet as I entered. He was a thin, dry sort of a man in slippers and a shabby grey suit and his hand seemed so small and delicate when I shook it that I wondered if he had really offered me all of its fingers.

227

'I'd like to know if you could christen my daughter?' I began.

'Are you a Catholic?' he asked, eyeing me up suspiciously.

'No, but I don't at all mind my daughter being christened a Catholic.'

'What religion do you belong to, then?'

'I suppose I was christened an Anglican, but I'm of an ecu-menical turn of mind.'

'Oh so am I, so am I. But this christening – I'm not exactly sure what the procedure is in these cases.'

He seemed to be addressing himself more to the bits of paper on his desk than to me, giving the impression that he was not overcome with enthusiasm for the project. It could well cause a lot more inconvenience than one small soul was worth. But for now he could be content with delaying tactics. 'I'm going to Granada on Friday,' he assured me, 'and I shall bring the matter up with the bishop then. Come and see me again next week.'

So I went to see Don Manuel the next week, but he hadn't made it to see the bishop, and the week after that he forgot to mention the business, and the week after that the bishop was going to think the matter over and the week after that I forgot all about it. So we somehow let it slide.

What I was conjuring in my mind was, in any case, not quite Don Manuel's way of doing things. I had an idea of a romantic little ceremony at an isolated country *ermita* or hermitage: Nuestra Señora de Fatima is a particularly pretty one, overlooking El Valero from the top of a steep cliff. I imagined a christening party setting out for the long climb to the *ermita* on a procession of gaily-caparisoned mules with flowers in their manes. Arriving at the chapel there would be a brief but charming service with candles and incense and the contented gurgling of the baby Chloë, then home again to gather around a long table with snow-white cloths, laden with glimmering glasses and mountains of mouthwatering food and wine.

The lugubrious deliberations of the bishop in his Granada fastness and Don Manuel's earnest profession of ecumenicism in his dark little office by the church seemed to be heading in the wrong direction. So Chloë started off her life without the help of orthodox religion and seemed to flourish reasonably well in its absence. Expira and Old Man Domingo, however, were clearly disappointed and for months would steer the conversation round to the deferred christening in the hopes of discovering a new date. And then it slipped from their minds as well.

~

Almost three years had passed when, one beautiful May morning, I found myself far from the known world on a botanising expedition, looking for plants from which to collect seeds in the summer. It was over towards Ventas de Zafarraya, wonderful seed-collecting country, miles from anywhere and locked in by soaring cliffs. I clambered and scrambled up and up along a goat-path, suicidally close to the fearful drop.

It was high, the air was thin and difficult to breathe, and it was as hot as a baking mountain can be in Andalucia in May. Reaching a spot where surely no man had ever trod before me, I was surprised, not to say a little piqued, to see a white-haired figure crouched in silent enchantment at the beauty of an iris. So lost in adoration was he that he didn't even hear me as I gasped and scuffled my way towards him.

At last he looked up from his reverie and, seeing me, slowly unfurled to his full six-feet-four. 'Buenos dias,' I said.

'Oh . . . do you speak English?'

'Not only that but I am English.'

'Marvellous. How delightful it is to meet fellow Englishmen in faraway places. Richard, Richard Blakeway-Phillips, and very pleased to meet you.'

We shook hands.

'Perhaps you saw me, but I've been admiring a most beautiful iris. It's either *xiphium* or *filifolia*; it's often quite difficult to tell them apart.'

'Well, we'll soon sort that out. I just happen to have Polunin with me.'

'Ah, Polunin. Thank heavens for that, we're saved.'

Anybody who has ever looked up a flower in a botany book will know the name of Oleg Polunin. Even the most accomplished botanist would consider it foolish to venture outside their front door without one of Polunin's tomes beneath their arm. No matter where you go in the world, Polunin will have been there before you and identified, catalogued and described in meticulous detail the indigenous flora. He is one of the most prodigious and respected botanists of the twentieth century. He was also my biology teacher at school, where he was known as Ollie Pollie. I regret to say that I was not a natural biologist and, having no notion of just what an honour it was to be taught by the great man, frittered away the privilege by horsing around at the back of the lab. Now that through almost daily use I've come to know Polunin's work, I am suitably wracked with remorse.

Richard flipped with practised skill through the countless pages of the book and mumbled as he ran his finger along the relevant entry.

'Of course, the gold centre blotches on the falls – *chamaeiris* – silly of us. I suppose it was rather foolish of me to come up here unarmed so to speak . . .'

'Unarmed?'

'I mean with no Polunin.'

I chatted on about the botanist and my early school experiences, ending wistfully with my wish of meeting him again, though I could hardly suppose this would be mutual.

'I think it would be a little difficult for you to meet him now,' said Richard with what I thought was a censorious look. 'He died several years ago.'

So we fell to lamenting this loss, high among the tutubias and the genista and the cistus, and the *Iris xiphium*, no, *filifolia*, while poring over Polunin. At such moments I love being English. I almost expected Richard to say, 'Would you care for a cup of tea?

230

I just happen to have with me my tea-service and some Lapsang Souchong.' But he didn't, and it was the wrong time of day for tea anyway. I kept my sweaty leather wine-bottle out of sight. It seemed somehow to be letting the side down.

Richard, or more properly the Reverend Richard Blakeway-Phillips, had been a vicar in the Midlands, but now he was retired and his great love was wandering the world botanising. That got me thinking, and as I darted to and fro, beelike, among the flowers and bushes, gathering specimens for identification and stuffing them unscientifically into my bag, my thoughts returned to the all but forgotten business of the christening.

I steered the conversation in the general direction of retired vicars and home christenings, and then enthused about the interesting botany to be found in the Alpujarras.

'We have a guest cottage on our farm. Maybe you'd like to come and stay, and while you were there perhaps you could christen our daughter.'

'Well, I must say,' said Richard, loosening his tie a little to combat the heat. 'It does sound very tempting – and I should be delighted to christen your daughter.'

So the deal was done and I hurried home to tell Ana, feeling pretty pleased with myself.

Within a fortnight Richard arrived on the bus from Granada with his wife Eleanor. He folded himself neatly into the back of the Landrover like a huge grasshopper, while Eleanor sat in the front and did the talking. She had accompanied Richard halfway around the world on his botanising adventures and had a habit of competently and discreetly taking care of each new situation they found themselves in. Without Richard's realising it, she acted as a forerunner, smoothing mountains into molehills and thus making possible such interesting undertakings as botanising in anarchic Albania, travelling on the local buses.

Eleanor was elegant, too. Whereas Richard did not place his appearance high on his list of priorities – he would wear a huge pair of tennis shoes, long shorts and a shirt with the collar askew and a tie draped somewhere between neck and breastbone – Eleanor achieved quite unconsciously an air of natural grace, as if instead of slogging up some dusty mountain track, she was hostessing a party on the vicarage lawn.

Chloë, for some reason better known perhaps to three-year-olds, had taken against the idea of the holy water and oil when we had explained it to her. This of course is the problem with leaving the business until the child has a will of its own. She flicked her head ominously and made it clear she didn't want to hear another word on the subject. Ana wrung her hands and looked at me appealingly. 'It'll probably be alright on the night,' I assured her. 'You know the way these things are.' I took refuge in my habitual optimism.

Introduced at lunch, Chloë regarded Richard and Eleanor with suspicion. They were, after all, very tall and imposing, and when they tried to weaken her defences by treating her as if she were a fellow human and by being nice to her, she sought refuge in silence. The next day, however, she was persuaded to accompany our guests down to the valley to give them a botanical tour. She was good at this; it gave her an opportunity to regurgitate the litany of botanical names she had learned on our seed-picking expeditions. But quite apart from revelling in sing-song Latin, she had a real love of plants and a good knowledge of the poisonous ones, which Ana had instilled in her before she could walk.

To non-botanists, the sound of a three-year-old trilling out names like *Adenocarpus decorticans*, *Euphorbia characias* or *Anthyllis cytisusoides* might seem monstrously precocious – though

232

city children are just as fluent with the names of favourite dinosaurs. In any case, we doting parents thought it was marvellous, and Richard and Eleanor, to whom such names were as bread and milk, were roundly impressed. The discovery of their shared enthusiasm for plants broke the ice, and when they returned to the house both factions seemed charmed by one another. I was dispatched to buy the ingredients for a giant paella and to inform the previously warned guests that all was in readiness for the following Saturday.

Susanne, a friend from the other side of town, was to be the godmother. She, like Domingo, was another person we wanted to draw into our family orbit. She had come to be a neighbour of ours as a result, so she said, of sticking a pin in a map of Europe and then moving lock, stock and barrel to the point thus decided upon. Like Georgina, she is one of those formidable young Englishwomen who steer their chosen course through the world quite oblivious of navigational hazards. Susanne is a gifted artist; she wanders the Alpujarra in her reprehensible wreck of a car, doing landscapes in pen and watercolour. As with astrologers, there is no shortage of artists in the Alpujarras, but Susanne's work, in its originality and the exquisite skill of its execution, holds its own with the best.

For the last few years Susanne has been confined to a wheelchair, due to crippling rheumatoid arthritis, but along with a disarming sultriness, she manages to maintain her unshakeable good humour. In her dark smoky voice she explained to me how the wretched disease was the result of unspeakable transgressions in earlier lives, something to do with supplying cosmetics containing white lead to the ladies of Minoan Crete, in the full knowledge of its harmful properties. Her eyes twinkled with delight as she growled out this singular story.

Chloë adores Susanne, because she is one of those people who are never too busy or too tired or in too much pain to fool around with children. She is one of the few foreigners in the Alpujarras whom I visit regularly, and she can always make me laugh. Anyway, the day before the christening, Domingo and I helped Susanne onto the back of the patient Bottom and waded with her across the river. Ana had had to leave early to collect her parents who were staying at a holiday apartment on the coast and, instead of waiting for the return of the Landrover, Susanne opted to process by donkey up to the house – the only guest to realise my more romantic plans for the christening.

I had also invited some friends from the town, along with Cathy and John and half their neighbours from Puerto Jubiley. Wherever Cathy and John go, half the villagers go along for the ride – but never more than half. There are two opposing factions in the village as the result of some fifty-year-old dispute concerning a poplar tree and a goat, and only one of the factions can be accommodated at any one time. For the christening we had the west of the river faction. Old Man Domingo and Expira were of course going to attend in their official capacity of god-grandparents; and then there were Bernardo and Isabel with their children, Fabian, Maite, and Chloë's beloved Rosa. Antonia, who by this time had become a very special friend of the family, was in Holland for an exhibition and so unable to come. In lieu of her presence she had sent Chloë a tiny sheep cast in bronze.

Along with Ana's mother and father, that made about forty people. So I borrowed two huge paella dishes and lit a great fire of rosemary and olive over which I placed the tripods. All morning the fire blazed away, scenting the breeze with its sweet smoke. The kitchen was cluttered with helpers making salads and dishes of dainties, and a great tub of fruity *costa* punch made its appearance. Somehow we gathered enough chairs and tables and cable drums for the company and Ana decked them with the snowy cloths I had dreamed of, setting arrangements of wild flowers on each table. Meanwhile Chloë played happily with

234

Rosa and the accursed Barbies, composing new episodes in the dolls' lives to accommodate the bronze sheep, blissfully unaware of the preparations.

At last the guests started to arrive, parking their cars by the bridge and scuffing up the dusty hill in their finery. The older members of the party who didn't fancy the trudge up to El Valero were ferried up the track in the Landrover. I placed the paellas on the fire and the drinks began to flow.

The Spanish contingent watched fascinated as Richard made adjustments to his robes. The older guests had little inkling of our religious persuasions and were perhaps expecting some sort of pagan rite. They shuffled carefully into a position from where they could bolt if things got out of control. With cries of '*a la misa*', I managed to gather the English and a few of the bolder Spaniards round the altar, a consecrated cable-drum with embroidered cloth and flowers, and quieten them enough for Richard to give a moving and simple address and read some prayers.

'Why don't you translate what he's saying so everybody can understand it?' Ana whispered.

'Because I'm overcome by the gravity of the moment, Ana,' I lied. The truth was that I didn't have the necessary apparatus connected for simultaneous translation from Biblical English to Alpujarran Spanish.

Chloë was persuaded to abandon Rosa and the dolls for a while and step forward in her party dress with Domingo and Susanne. She was a robust, reluctant and slippery toddler, so the godparents had to dispense with the tradition of carrying the infant tenderly to the font, and stand awkwardly beside her instead. Chloë looked as if she was about to cut up rough but Ana managed to bribe her into a hesitant co-operation by flashing the edge of a bar of chocolate, kept at the ready in her pocket, and pointing meaningfully towards the altar. Chloë

235

edged forward throwing side glances at the chocolate in the way that sailors keep a lighthouse in view when crossing onshore tides.

Richard looked magnificent in his beautiful robes, standing in the dappled sunlight beneath the acacia tree. He bent down and placed his hand gently on Chloë's shoulder, uttered the appropriate incantation and made the sign of the cross with the holy water and oil on her scrunched-up brow. Ana and I breathed a sigh of relief as she slunk back to Rosa clutching her chocolate. I like to think they shared it. It's no good just going through with the form of the thing, you have to act by its precepts.

As a climax to the service, and to the utter bafflement of the Spanish faction, the English then sang 'All Things Bright And Beautiful', this being the only hymn in which we could all pass muster. Chorus, then first verse, then chorus again, then a verse that Richard had written specially for the occasion, then a last chorus. Unaccompanied and a little wobbly at the start, the communal voices soon gathered in strength and soared across the valley, their song swelled by the rushing of the rivers and the call of a nightingale ringing out from the *barranco*.

WATER OVER THE BRIDGE . . .

DURING OUR FIRST YEARS AT EL VALERO THE WEATHER HAD
been more or less predictable. The summers were hot and the
winters were mild. Although a feeling of nervous anticipation
would set in when we contemplated the onset of the fierce summer heat, we were surprised, when it actually happened, by how
well we adapted to it. We soon learned to drag the bed onto the
roof and sleep beneath the stars, to hang a heavy blanket over the
door to keep the cool air in the house, and to put a bottle of
frozen water in the struggling gas fridge. Winter weather was
comfortable, cool and sunny, though with not quite enough rain
to keep the flora of the hills in good fettle. Even during our own
short time here we had noticed that the winters had seemed to
become just slightly drier – nothing dramatic but enough to
leave an air of dejection about the trees and a desperation
among the more shallow-rooted plants.

The river ran on easily and inoffensively through winter and
summer alike, swelling briefly as the June heat melted the moun-

tain snow, then returning to its lazy summer level. The rain and the river muddled along in their own way, apparently reluctant to give us any trouble, until the summer after Chloë's christening when we had our first taste of serious drought.

Almost no snow had fallen that winter on the mountains, and the spring rains fell feebly and dried up with a spate of hot winds coming up from the Sahara. By June the river was no more than a few brackish puddles among the boulders, and then in July, for the first time in living memory, the trickle of water in the Cádiar river stopped altogether.

Dead fish lay rotting in the dry pools and the paths of the valley were ankle-deep in hot dust. The grass in the fields at El Valero withered to brown and crackled beneath our feet, and the leaves of the trees shrivelled and curled. On hot summer evenings in previous years we would stroll *en famille* down to the ford, and bathe in the pool, or sit enjoying the breeze and watching the swallows and bats put on their evening aerobatic show; but that summer it was difficult to imagine water ever running again in the river. The silence of the river was made more sinister by the insane screaming of the cicadas.

It's the Greenhouse Effect, said some . . . the hole in the ozone layer . . . El Niño . . . an unfortunate alignment of planets. The old men shook their heads and predicted dark times to come. The drought affected the whole of Andalucía and most of Spain. Rivers and springs dried up all over the province; wells were down to the salty sludge at the bottom; whole forests of trees, even the hardy Aleppo pines, withered and died. Órgiva was limited to an hour of water a day, and there were bush-fires breaking out right across Spain.

238

~

Ana and I felt somehow let down by the river. We had bought our farm on its far side – cheap, because nobody else wanted to take the risk – and during all of our time here the river had been nothing but a good neighbour to us, entertaining us during the day and lulling us to sleep at night. It had left our bridges alone, it had permitted us to drive the Landrover through the ford at most times of the year, and it provided cool bathing to refresh us from the heat, and clear water to irrigate our crops. It showed none of the nasty tendencies we had been warned about – and now it had gone and dried up.

I had found the idea of living close to a really dangerous and elemental force rather appealing but it had become about as elemental as a duck-pond in a municipal park. It was a dying thing, it seemed. When I mentioned these thoughts to Domingo or his parents, they would shake their heads and look at me in consternation. Nonetheless, as September arrived and there was no sign of the thunderstorms that come to break the summer heat, people grew more and more concerned.

As if to compound the misery, towering banks of thunderheads would gather around the mountains, and then black clouds would boil up the valley, but not a drop of rain fell. As night drew on, the stars would appear through the gaps in the cloud and by the time midnight came the sky would be clear once again. Perhaps this really was a fundamental weather change.

A number of foreigners thought this was the case and talked of abandoning their Andalucian homes. Barkis's rescuers, George and Alison, who live high up on the Contraviesa, were thinking of moving north to rain-sodden Galicia. They had created a water-garden with a pool and waterfall, right beside their house, but the spring that supplied its stream had dried up the year before and now there was barely enough water for the rabbits.

Moving away was hardly an option for us, as we had already burnt our boats by buying a farm that no one else was likely to want. It was a relief, though, not to have to bother ourselves about that decision. Like Domingo, we would be staying come

239

fair weather or foul, and the knowledge that this was so served to strengthen the bonds between us.

Then in mid-September it rained. A few heavy drops fell, sporadically at first, each one making a small crater in the dust. Little by little the drops coalesced into a steady drizzle. The colour of the land darkened and the air filled with the smell of hot wet dust and pine. The stones in the river glistened and with the passing of the hours tiny rivulets and puddles began to form. A quiet sussuration became apparent where before there had been silence. By the morning, still with no heavy rain, the river was flowing again. With the lowering of the clouds everybody's spirits started to lift. It rained lightly for three days, enough to settle the dust and build up the flow of the river, and then it stopped. Everybody agreed that there had not been enough rain to water even the peppers, and that the time for rejoicing had not yet come.

September moved into October with no more rain, though something kept the river going. And then in November the downfall began, not with a deluge, just a nice steady downpour that kept on coming day and night, day and night. By the morning of the second day there was a terrifying flow of dark water racing down from the gorge. Effortlessly it shifted the bridge out of the way, pulverising the stone piers and sweeping the beams far down the river. And with each passing hour it rose still more, bringing with it boulders the size of small buildings thundering like cannons as they moved through the awful tumult. The water was black and evil-smelling, and all the country round, normally so quiet, echoed to its monstrous noise.

The days of rain became weeks and our roof started to leak, the solar power died, and all the firewood was so soaked it was useless. The river thundered on, filling the valley with a sense of foreboding. As the earth became saturated with water, the hills began to crumble into the valleys. We would hear a roar and watch as hundreds of tons of sodden earth and rocks avalanched down the mountainside, bringing trees and bushes along with it. Much of the *acequia* was destroyed by landslips so that there was not even a trace of its former path, and a huge mass of rock had slithered down onto the track. The only way to get things up to the house now was with the wheelbarrow. I had never imagined such awesome erosion; the mountains were literally being swept down to the sea.

We had no telephone, which had the effect of emphasising our isolation, though we were also pleased not to be worrying people by telling them how awful things had become. There were fourteen buckets and bowls dotted about the house catching drips, and the nearest thing to good cheer was a dull fire smouldering in the chimney.

Ana, with her usual foresight, had amassed a decent stock of tinned tomatoes and dried pasta to eat, some potatoes, onions and flour, custard powder and anchovies, but there was little else. We weaved around the drips in the house, trying to find amusements for Chloë and distractions from the minor ailments that were beginning to plague us; coughs, sniffles, wheezy chests and a lassitude that the damp pages of Juliette and a water-logged herb garden could do little to alleviate.

I remembered Expira and Old Man Domingo's warnings about the river and their dread tales of the Deaf One's daughter dying in childbirth, or the woman with acute appendicitis whose mule was swept from beneath her when she tried to reach the hospital. So this was what they had been talking about.

There was a way out from El Valero if an emergency arose but it involved a four-hour walk up the hill and along to Mecina Fondales. The bridge at Mecina was an ancient stone one built fifty feet above the river in a narrow gorge and usable at any state of flood. This way might have been an option for shopping, at a pinch, but less useful in cases of appendicitis.

As our enforced isolation continued, we became daily more disheartened and began to feel a little threatened by the ceaseless roaring of waters and the rain and mist that now never left the valley. Under normal circumstances we would do all we could to avoid going to town, but now we were almost reduced to tears by the thought of its unattainable delights.

And then one day as I was wandering about down by the river, I saw Domingo. What struck me about his presence was that he was on our side of the river. When I had finished expressing my astonishment, he told me that he had managed to walk across in a place where the river was wider and shallower, using a stout stick to support himself. He had just come to check that we were alright. 'What we need to do is fix up a cable across the river,' he announced. 'It's never been done here before because people are too old-fashioned to think of anything new, but I think it could be the solution to your problems.'

The next morning I stood on the bank of the river just upstream from the ford, waiting while Domingo sorted out a tangle of string and wire on the far side. After several tries he managed to throw across a stone attached to a line of string. I pulled on the string and steadily the wire cable passed over the river. On the wire was a bag containing a spanner and a pair of bulldog clips. I passed the cable around the base of the trunk of a stout bush and connected it with the bulldog clips.

When I had finished, Domingo connected his end to the trunk of a tamarisk, in a similar manner to my side but including a tensioning screw, which he then wound up as tight as he could. Then he snapped a shackle onto the cable, and, suspended beneath it on a rope, inched out across the water. The cable stretched as he reached the middle but he was still a good metre

242

above the river, and in less than a minute he landed among the bushes on our side.

I clapped him on the back and laughed for sheer relief that he was safe, and delight that the thing was going to work. We then set to work putting in a couple more tensioning screws and reinforcing the anchor around the bush, and within the hour we had a safe and serviceable aerial cableway that we could use until the river dropped enough to build a new bridge.

Over the following weeks we refined the 'Flying Fox' with a smooth-running system of ropes and pulleys, a comfortable canvas bucket-seat, and a landing platform on either side of the river. Its only small disadvantage was that, except for those with a very outward bound sort of disposition, you needed two people to make it work, thus reducing the already thin incidence of single visitors. Chloë loved to be hauled across; it was the best swing she has ever known. We all got pretty skilled at using it, passing across gas-bottles, sacks of animal-feed, sacks of shopping, a new water-tank, friends and neighbours and their children, some rams, and, on one occasion, a sick ibex.

The ibex had been found hiding in a bush by the ford one evening. It was stricken with the sarcoptic mange, a skin disease that the wild ibexes had picked up from flocks of sheep and goats. At the time the mange was sweeping through the ibex population and causing great concern to the Nature Protection Agency. Domingo suggested that we haul it across the river and take it to 243 the Agency vet in town. We caught it, lashed the poor creature's feet together and hung it from the shackle. Then we swung it across the river and dumped it in the back of Pepe's Landrover, to the consternation of his dogs who were crammed to one side to make room. The vet bathed the ibex, vaccinated it and then released it a week later fully recovered. It took poor Pepe another week, however, to rid his dogs of the scourge.

~

When the rain finally stopped and the clouds lifted, we set about drying out the house, a matter of dragging outside anything that could be lifted and flinging open the doors and windows to let the sun and wind blast through. Then we began picking up the threads of our daily life. One afternoon, as I was hacking the finishing touches to a drainage channel from the sodden stableyard, I was surprised to see Antonia walking up the path.

'Hello,' she said in her carefully intoned English. 'I have brought something for you people all alone with no bridge. See, here are some cakes – and this bottle, I think, will cheer you up.' It was always a pleasure to see Antonia and she was right about the Dutch gin, but it amazed me that she had appeared at all.

'How did you get across the river?' I asked. 'Don't tell me you can use the cable on your own?'

'Domingo helped me,' she answered simply. 'He will come and join us, he is making the cable more strong. He wants to borrow something.'

Sure enough, Domingo soon sauntered up the hill, casting critical glances at my attempts – too little and too late – to make flood channels. He sat down with us and drank some tea, a thing he very rarely does, and even helped himself to one of Antonia's cakes. Neither Ana nor I had ever known him to eat cake in our house before.

'I want to borrow the fencing pliers.'

'Of course. Why, what are you doing?'

'Putting up a bit of fencing to stop the sheep shitting on Antonia's terrace,' he replied as if it was a routine farming chore.

That autumn Antonia had moved into the house at La Herradura, just across the valley, to get away from the turmoil of the building of a new battery rabbit and chicken farm at La Hoya. The owner of La Herradura was pleased to have Antonia

244

living in the house at a peppercorn rent, as houses here seem to show their appreciation of a human presence by being slower to fall down. Domingo's flock, unable to cross the river, was grazing that winter at La Herradura, and the sheep, all two hundred of them, liked to gather in a tight huddle on Antonia's patio to shelter from the rain; hence the problem with the sheep-shit.

Domingo apparently needed to borrow a lot of tools for whatever it was that he was doing at La Herradura because he accompanied Antonia on almost all of her trips back and forth to the house. We grew used to seeing them walking together up to our patio and, if it surprised us that Domingo seemed rather more sociable than before, and Antonia somehow happier and more spirited, we neither of us felt inclined to comment on it.

By the middle of April the water level had gone down enough for us to build a new bridge. Domingo and I, with Bottom dragging the heavy green beams, built it in a short day, a considerable achievement I thought. I had no more illusions about its permanency. I had learned my lesson about building in the river. As the snow on the high mountains melted with the heat of early summer, the river rose again, giving the new bridge a battering, but leaving it this time where it was. Then the river settled down to its summer level, flowing peacefully down the valley. Having shown us its wrath, it was a good neighbour again.

245

The summer that followed the rains was a rather more auspicous season. The sheep thrived on the lush grasses that now covered the hill, giving us a fine yield of lambs. The holiday cottage that we called El Duque, the old name for the land on that side of the river, was occupied week after week by guests who were delighted with the beauty of the exuberantly blooming countryside. Our seed-merchant friend from Sussex came to stay, bringing a huge order for scores of different varieties, and the plants that were to bear the seeds responded to the mood of optimism by flowering in spectacular fashion. We felt ready for anything.

In September Chloë was due to start school. She was not quite four but Rosa had started the year before and Chloë was desperate to join her. She felt none of the trepidation of her parents about her coming ordeal. The day your first child starts school is a staging post of life, one of the many leaps into the abyss. We were horribly wistful at the thought of our only daughter lurching away from us in the Órgiva school bus but tried to make a decent show of sharing her excitement at becoming a proper Spanish schoolgirl.

∼

August nights can be hot. You sit outside, scantily dressed for coolness, and the sweat still pours off you, while the frenzied screaming of the cicadas and other hot-night creatures makes your head reel.

That summer there was one spectacularly sultry night. Sleep would have been impossible so, after a late supper, we three – along with the two dogs – went down to the Cádiar for a midnight bathe. The moon was full to illuminate our path and we took some candles to light the shadows by the river.

246   There was a pool in the river which we had made by spanning the gap between a couple of rocks with some tree-trunks, and filling in the dam with stones and brushwood. We set the candles on the dam and slipped into the cool water. Swimming upstream a little, we drifted back with the lazy current and watched the moonlight and the candle-flames glittering in the ripples on the dark surface of the water. The canes and willows on the banks stood motionless in the breathless heat of the night. The dogs sat patiently by the water and Chloë, sitting like a mermaid on a

rock, droned sleepily on through a succession of Spanish nurs-ery rhymes that Rosa had taught her.

All of a sudden the dogs leapt to their feet and growled, staring into the distance up the river. The moon had sunk behind the Serreta now, and apart from the pool of light made by our can-dles, the river was in darkness. I shivered a little anxiously, won-dering what might be out there. We peered into the shadows but could see nothing. And then little by little a pale mist seemed to fill the valley. It swelled and then shrank, and then started to take on a more solid form as it moved closer towards us. We stood and stared, transfixed.

Bonka started to bark furiously, and then I heard the bells. It was Domingo's sheep moving down the moonlit river. I could just make out the tall shape of Bottom with her huge ears erect, at the head of the flock. As they drew closer I could make out Domingo riding the donkey; and behind him, with her arms around his waist and her head sleepy on his shoulder, was Antonia.

We slid like alligators back into the river and grinned at one another as they passed.

ACKNOWLEDGMENTS

Thanks to Natania Jansz and Mark Ellingham, my editors and publishers, for their encouragement, advice and friendship. They must at times have regretted the day we first sat munching oranges beside the river, discussing a book – but if they did, they never let it show. Thanks also to Carole Stewart and Andrew Hogg for helping this book and its author along in a hundred different ways; to Domingo and his family; to Antonia and 'los del Puerto' for their unstinting friendship and neighbourly help; and to the ever-inspiring, ever-welcoming Ortega family, who run the *Bar Mirasierra*, my 'office' in Órgiva. Above all, of course, warmest thanks to Ana and Chloë, who have put up with me, curbed my excesses, stopped me getting uppity, and provided so much of the material that you have just read.

249

A TUSCAN CHILDHOOD

by Kinta Beevor

When Kinta Beevor was five years old, her father, the painter Aubrey Waterfield, bought the sixteenth-century Fortezza della Brunella in the Tuscan village of Aulla. There her parents were part of a vibrant artistic community that included Aldous Huxley, Bernard Berenson, and D. H. Lawrence. Meanwhile, Kinta and her brother explored the countryside, helped with the grape and olive harvests, and came to know and love the charming Italian people. Lyrical and witty, *A Tuscan Childhood* is alive with the timeless splendor of Italy.

Travel/Europe/0-375-70426-4

IRELAND IN MIND

Edited and with an introduction by Alice Leccese Powers

From Oscar Wilde to James Joyce, from Virginia Woolf to Frank McCourt: three centuries of fiction, poems, and essays, from both Irish expatriates and non-Irish visitors in search of the real Ireland. For travelers of all kinds, for those who have long been fascinated by Ireland and those who are feeling its lure for the first time, *Ireland in Mind* will provide a rich and rewarding imaginative journey. Contributors also include Samuel Beckett, Paul Theroux, Wallace Stevens, Jonathan Swift, and George Bernard Shaw.

Travel/Europe/0-375-70344-6

ITALY IN MIND

Edited and with an introduction by Alice Leccese Powers

From Lord Byron and Edith Wharton to Susan Sontag and Michael Ondaatje—two centuries of writers celebrate their love affairs with Italy. Comprised of short stories, novel excerpts, essays, poetry, journal entries, and letters, *Italy in Mind* captures all the contradictions of the Italian scene: enduring tradition and trendy consumerism, ravishing landscapes and urban sprawl, demonic bureaucracy and unvanquishable human warmth. The result is a work of enchantment, a tribute both to Italy and to generations of literary travelers.

Travel/Europe/0-679-77023-2

A YEAR IN PROVENCE

by Peter Mayle

In this witty and warm-hearted book, Peter Mayle realizes a long-cherished dream and moves into a 200-year-old stone farmhouse in the remote country of the Lubéron with his wife and two large dogs. He endures January's frosty mistral as it comes howling down from the Rhône Valley, discovers the secrets of goat racing through the middle of town, and delights in the glorious regional cuisine. In this enchanting and often hilarious book, Mayle transports us into all the earthy pleasures of Provençal life and lets us live vicariously at a tempo governed by seasons, not by days.

Travel/Europe/0-679-73114-8

TOUJOURS PROVENCE

by Peter Mayle

Taking up where his beloved *A Year in Provence* leaves off, Peter Mayle offers us another funny and beautifully evocative book about life in Provence. With tales only one who lives there could know—of finding old gold coins while digging in the garden, of indulging in sumptuous feasts at truck stops—and characters introduced with great affection and wit, *Toujours Provence* is a delicious and irresistible portrait of a place where, if you can't quite "get away from it all," you can surely have the best of times trying.

Travel/Europe/0-679-73604-2

ENCORE PROVENCE

New Adventures in the South of France

by Peter Mayle

For a time, Francophile extraordinaire Peter Mayle left the South of France, but not a day passed without a pang of loneliness for the home he had left behind. And so he returned and fell in love all over again with *la vie Provençale*. In *Encore Provence*, he gives us a glimpse into the nuances of the truffle trade, a parfumerie lesson on the delicacies of scent, and an exploration of the genetic effects of 2,000 years of foie gras. Here, too, are Mayle's latest tips on where to find the best honey, cheese, or *chambre d'hôte* the region has to offer.

Travel/Europe/0-679-76269-8

DINNER WITH PERSEPHONE
Travels in Greece
by Patricia Storace

A *New York Times* Notable Book of the Year

Brilliantly mixing affection with detachment, rapture with clarity, this American poet perfectly evokes a country delicately balanced between East and West. Whether she is interpreting Hellenic dream books, pop songs, and soap operas, describing breathtakingly beautiful beaches and archaic villages, or braving the crush at a saint's tomb, Storace rewards the reader with informed and sensual insights into Greece's soul. Passionate and stylish, funny and erudite, *Dinner with Persephone* is travel writing elevated to a fine art.

Travel/Europe/0-679-74478-9

ON PERSEPHONE'S ISLAND
A Sicilian Journal
by Mary Taylor Simeti

When Mary Taylor Simeti first came to Sicily, she intended to make just a short visit. Instead, she stayed for over twenty years. With both a native's intimacy and the fresh eye of an outsider, she chronicles a year in the place she calls Persephone's Island. Simeti navigates through Sicily's history of Greek, Arab, Norman, and Spanish conquests. She savors the fruits of its harvests. At once poetic and precise, learned and deeply personal, *On Persephone's Island* is an absorbing account of a place imbued with sounds, tastes, colors, and myth.

Travel/Europe/0-679-76414-3